THE 5 PHASES OF DATING

✦ ☆ ✦

The Grown-Ass Woman's Guide to Attracting and Maintaining Authentic Relationships

✦ ☆ ✦

Anita M. Charlot

Relationship Architect Academy
1116 Garfield Street
Suite #1522
Oak Park, Illinois 60304

Anita M. Charlot

THE 5 PHASES OF DATING
The Grown-Ass Woman's Guide to Attracting and Maintaining Authentic Relationships

Copyright© 2017 by Anita M. Charlot.

All rights reserved. Printed in the United States of America. No part of this book may be reproduced or transmitted in any form or by any means, electronic or mechanical, including photocopying, recording, or by any information storage and retrieval system, without written permission from the publisher. For information, send your inquiry to:

Relationship Architect Academy; 1116 Garfield Street, Suite #1522, Oak Park, IL 60304

The intent of the author is for inspirational and informational purposes only. The CONTENT in this book is not intended to be a substitute for professional medical advice, diagnosis, or treatment. Always seek the advice of your physician or other qualified mental health provider with any questions you may have regarding a medical condition. Never disregard professional medical advice or delay in seeking it because of something you have read in this book.

This BOOK does not offer diagnosis and or treatment for medical or mental conditions. You must consult with your own doctors in determining if the methodologies suggested in this BOOK are appropriate for you and your conditions.

The 5 Phases Of Dating

In the event you use any of the information in the book for yourself, which is your constitutional right, the author and the publisher assume no responsibility for your actions.

ISBN: 978-0-9708031-6-0

Relationship Architect Academy and Anita Charlot; All Rights Reserved

Learn more about Anita and her offerings at
www.anitacharlot.com

Learn more about the Relationship Architect Academy
www.relationshiparchitectacademy.com

Anita M. Charlot

DEDICATION

I dedicate this book to all my clients, students, and social media followers for allowing me to continue to share my passion, my personal dating and relationship experiences as well as over twenty years of dating and relationship coaching practice. May you first find yourself in these pages, do the work to heal your heart, and attract and maintain your very own authentic relationship just like I have.

To my daughters of love Bianca and Ariana, I may not have given birth to you, but I want both of you to continue to grow into knowing who you are, accept the truth about yourselves, and then create a life full of moments that make love to your heart as often as possible. Whether you know it or not, this book will set you on the path of not wasting years of your life in unfulfilling relationships and will teach you how to find your voice to create the relationships you **really** want, even if they didn't start out that way.

To my niece Crystal, thank **you** for being the role model **I needed** to set me on the right path and for choosing my nephew-in-law to light the way…**I love you girl**! And to all the young girls and women that find it in their heart to call me "Mom," I so appreciate you. I do not take the fact that you call me Mom lightly; it is truly an honor. This book is for you too!

Anita M. Charlot

To my sons, dudes…you've been around me long enough to have witnessed the pain, the heartache, and the disappointment I have experienced throughout the years. I am so glad you are now able to witness the quality of love I currently have. You now have an example of what a loving and truly authentic relationship looks like. Lord **knows** I'm grateful for that on so many levels. May you one day find yourself in a loving and authentic relationship that feeds your heart, makes you feel safe, and supports you beyond measure. In the meantime, work on being the best **you** that you can be, not only for yourselves, but also for your relationships.

Mom, girl…I love you with all my heart. It is because of you that I have grown into the woman that I am today. May you gain a deeper understanding of my dating and relationship journey and the passion I have for making sure that other women (and a few smart men) get it right.

To my girls, Edwina, Laurie, and Krys, I don't know how I would have weathered the storms without you. Thank you all for being there for me through running nightmares, the nights hugging the porcelain God, the granny flowered dresses, and wiping away the tears and being ready to open an old fashioned can of "whip ass" if I ever needed it.

And last, but not least, thank you to the man that elevated the dating and relationship game for me. The man who saw through the tough exterior and fell in love with me **because** of my past, provided me a safe space to grow through my fears and insecurities, accepted my children as his own, and continues to support **all** my entrepreneurial

The 5 Phases Of Dating

pursuits and intuitively **knew** how I needed to be loved to blossom into the woman I am today. It's because of you, my love, that I know no matter what my past experience has been, it is possible to have the quality of love far beyond what I could have ever imagined for myself. May the path that **we** have created light the way for other women all over the world, especially our daughters. Love check…got it right here for you baby!

Anita M. Charlot

The 5 Phases Of Dating

TABLE OF CONTENTS

✻ ☆ ✻

FOREWORD   xv
PREFACE   xix

INTRODUCTION   1
  My Dating and Relationship History   7
  Dedication of Your Purrfectly Authentic™ Journal (Paj)   15

PART 1:
INTERNAL GROUNDWORK: GETTING IN TOUCH WITH YOUR PURRFECTLY AUTHENTIC™ SELF   15
  DEFINING YOUR PURRFECTLY AUTHENTIC™ RELATIONSHIP   16
  PURRFECTLY AUTHENTIC VOCABULARY   17
  YOUR THREE LISTS: MUST HAVES, CAN COMPROMISE ONS, AND HELL NAWS!   22
  WAIT…WHAT? I THOUGHT WE WERE IN A RELATIONSHIP?!?!   24
  THE 3-6-9 RULE   26

Exercise: 28
In your journal, answer these questions 28

PART 2:
THE 5 PHASES OF DATING 31

PHASE I:
FRIENDSHIP -LOCATING THE DESIRED NEIGHBORHOOD 33

Proposed Timeline 34
What You See Is What You Get 34
Evaluation Time! 35
Where Are They Now? 35
Discussion of *The 5 Phases* Of Dating 37
Too Much Information (Tmi) 42
The Importance of Integrity 45
Keep Both Eyes Open 47
Understanding a Person's Energy/Spirit 48
Respect of Time and Space 49
The Bus Stops Here 50

The 5 Phases Of Dating

PHASE II:
DATING, BUT NOT EXCLUSIVELY - SURVEYING THE LANDSCAPE   51

   Proposed Timeline: 3-6 Months   52

   All Dating Situations Are Not Potential Relationships!!!   52

   Interview Phase   53

   Dating Multiple People?   55

   Keep Shopping   58

   Me Time   60

   Creating the Blueprint   61

   Deceptive Advertising   62

   The Reality of Finances   65

   Money Talks   68

   Let's Talk Honesty   69

   Doing Your Research   73

   Cat/Dog Theory   74

   Leave the Drama At The Door   75

   If The Train Doesn't Stop At Your Station, Then It's Not Your Train!!!   76

   Let It Go!   77

PHASE III:

DATING EXCLUSIVELY - A COMMITTED RELATIONSHIP - LAYING THE FOUNDATION

	87
Answering the Phone or Door	88
Living Arrangements	89
Communication	93
Accessing Email/Voicemail	94
Stay True To You!	96
What's Yours Is Yours; what's Theirs Is Theirs	98
Your Friends versus Our Friends	99
Flipping the Script	99
Advance or Retreat	105
Take Care Of You!	106

PHASE IV:

ENGAGEMENT - PLANNING A LIFE TOGETHER - BUILDING THE HOUSE   109

R-E-S-P-E-C-T Your Relationship	110
"Deceptive Advertising 2.0"	116
Living Arrangements	117
Your Junk...My Junk	118
Continue To Feed Your Spirit	120
The Balancing Act of Compromise	122

    Being Supportive Versus Being Overbearing   124

PHASE V:
MARRIAGE OR LIFETIME COMMITMENT - LEARNING, LOVING, AND GROWING TOGETHER   129
    Communication   130
    Choosing Your Battles   132
    Improve Each Other   133
    Everyone Else...Butt Out!!!   133
    Never Lose Sight Of Who You Are As An Individual!!!   135

PART 4:
DIFFERENCES BETWEEN DATING AS A WOMAN VS. A GROWN-ASS WOMAN   137

FINAL THOUGHTS   159
AFTERWORD   165

Anita M. Charlot

The 5 Phases Of Dating

FOREWORD

✯ ☆ ✯

Girl...

It's been twelve years since the original *5 Phases* was published. To say that I am overjoyed that it was relevant then, and is still relevant, would be an understatement. Though times change, people-in general- do not. We are who we are. *The 5 Phases* is 'Nit's story as much as it is mine... and continues to be as we grow through the branches of our mighty oaks called Life.

"Love from within. To withhold it from others is to withhold it from myself. If I give it to everyone, then I'm never out of love's presence" (Charlot, 2007). She probably doesn't even remember saying that to me, amongst the millions of snippets of advice I sought from her over the nearly twenty years we've been attached in spirit... and in harsh truths. That saying applied then... and resonates with me now since I am prone to disconnect from humans very quickly when they don't seem to be in alignment with **my** plan. *The 5 Phases* has served as a cathartic (and, for OCD me, pragmatic) approach to not cutting "people off at the knees" quite so much. It has helped me to be much more methodical in my approach to dating-recognizing that I am the **only** one responsible for **my** happiness. Imagine that ish! What a concept!!!{mind more than slightly blown here}

I also am reminded of the dedications in the original release....those 'Nit made to her beloved sons,

Gerald and BJ, and to her goddaughter, Bianca. She thanked them for trusting her relationship decisions and their unconditional love for her regarding her choice of partners-especially since the choices were often untraditional and unconventional in society's purview. Again, this is as relevant then, as it is now. *(Pouring out a little for my homie, Charles-with his fine ass-here....who has loved her 'dirty drawers' as we like to say as proof of someone who's down for you regardless!)*

In typical 'Nit fashion, she also dedicated the original to someone who was the love of her life, and gave her the space and inclination to pursue her dream of writing. We all were super grateful for that type of love. (Spoiler alert-proceed with caution because shit starts to get 'really real' midway through.)

With regards to my own life, I've read this damn book so much until the pages are a bit crumply from the spit on my fingers to turn them. The ends of my book curl upward from me clinching it when "mo-fo's" didn't fall into alignment with the Phase in mind! I re-read it for the hundredth time recently, trying to make sense of where my current interest derailed. The lessons stay the same, but our understanding of how we digest and apply them remain fluid. Yay team!

As the revised version hits bookstands-electronic and traditional alike-I am deliciously excited about where *The 5 Phases* will take 'Nit, but mostly where it will take her readers and their investments in being attuned to their wants, needs, and desires, even the funk-stank-nasty ones, that nobody ever wants to say out loud.

The 5 Phases Of Dating

As I raise my Tiffany & Co® champagne flute filled to the brim with mimosa, I toast to you. Here's to slinking sexily into your new and/or renewed sense of dating as you flow through the pages of *The 5 Phases of Dating: The Grown Ass Woman's Guide to Attracting and Maintaining Authentic Relationships*. Drops mic.

Your mirror and best friend for life,
Krys-Krys

Anita M. Charlot

PREFACE

☆

I must be honest with you, this isn't the first version of this book. I published a book by a very similar title in 2005 and have been meaning to update it ever since. My life was different back then. The publishing process was more expensive and my relationship situation was a tad bit rocky; however, I knew that I had to publish an updated version. Fast forward twelve years later, and I'm finally ready.

Since that first book, I've grown so much, mentally, spiritually, emotionally, relationally, and physically. I've accepted my good and my shadow side 100% unconditionally. I've identified the spirit of the person that is perfectly imperfect for me. I've watched my body morph into something that I could not even recognize; I've had hot flashes that seemed to last forever, and I have shifted directions in my business several times.

So why did I feel compelled to update **this** book, specifically for the grown-ass woman? It's because I have been coaching and teaching grown-ass women for over twenty years now, and it amazes me how many of these women are so unsuccessful in love. They have the look, the bank account, the investments, the education, their own businesses, and the fortitude to climb mountains in stilettoes **or** Timberlands, yet…they are still alone.

Why can't they find the love that they want? Why can't these women find men that will make love to their hearts way before they make love to their bodies? Why can't they find men interested in making love versus just having sex? I hear my clients, friends, and coworkers complaining that there are no good men out there, yet every day, there is a man that is running through hell, climbing mountains, and swimming out to the middle of the lake to let **his** woman know just how special she is. What sets this woman apart? What can be done? How do I reach the grown-ass woman who can't seem to find love?

While I admit, I spend a great amount of time on Facebook creating posts versus interacting via video, I can't reach **all** women that way. Writing this book is the best choice. Besides, if you know these women like I do, then you know that they will never admit publicly that they are crying themselves to sleep at night; or that they are pretending to be strong on the outside, while hiding the hurt little girl on the inside. I pray that the woman that picks up this book, finds herself in these pages, recognizes that she is not alone, and realizes no matter what her past relationship experience has been, she can still attract and maintain the relationship of her dreams. Just like I did!

Disclaimer: I want to prepare you for what you are about to discover. I will reveal parts of my life's past that you may or may not be aware of. Once discovered, you may immediately feel some type of way; that is your choice. However, I'd like to ask you to hold back on judgement, focus on the message, and don't let your personality get in the way of the message that your heart and spirit need to hear. In all honesty, what you will learn about me just proves the fact that I am probably the most experienced dating and relationship coach you will ever come across. I've earned my stripes, I love **all of me, and I stand in my truth.

So where did the concept of The 5 Phases of Dating come from? It was spring: the time of renewal and rebirth; the

The 5 Phases Of Dating

time of hope and inspiration; the time of new beginnings. Spring, the time of anticipation when new life emerges from the dormant seeds of winter ushering in the change of seasons. Sometimes, however, seeds of change leave us harvesting a difficult crop, and so it was for me in the spring of 2003.

This season of new beginnings was marked by a sad and painful end; my four-year relationship was over, and this season of rebirth took on a personal meaning. I sadly faced the reality that I was alone, and in my aloneness, I was not at all sure who I was, and I was much less certain about who I wanted to be, or who I was going to become for that matter.

My life plan was to love my partner until the end of time. "It's just me and you, everything else is just a movie," I would say. Oh, how I wanted to believe it! Had I been fooling myself into thinking that no matter what, we could overcome all obstacles? Had I ignored the signs in hopes that my deepest desires could be my reality? I now question whether we stayed together because of love, despite our obvious differences, or for the numerous other reasons that generally keep couples together.

We were comfortable. We shared a house because it was less frightening to be a partner with someone than to face the fear of being alone. So many questions came to mind, and I was determined to find answers. I not only wanted answers to these questions, but also answers to the many questions that popped into my head about love, relationships, dating, commitment, marriage, friendship, and life. See, I had lived, loved, and lost so much in the past that with the end of this partnership, I was determined to move beyond this barrier, which meant performing some internal reflection and answering difficult questions.

Would it not be easy to consider myself the angel and point my accusing finger at my ex-husband, former boyfriends, past partners, or the fathers of my children and allow myself to believe it was entirely their fault? That would be a lie. It took a long time for me to *see* the truth, even longer to *acknowledge* and accept what I saw, yet longer still to act and change it. During my time alone-my sabbatical, if you will-I learned a great deal about honesty, and for the first time, I understood *my* truths. I discovered my likes and dislikes, not the superficial, rehearsed ones that people ask about on an early date, where more than likely we haven't been honest from the beginning, but rather the truth deep down inside.

I examined my past relationships and began sifting through the debris left in their wake. I began to consider how I might have deceived myself, either in the beginning when I decided to enter the relationship, or in the end when I hesitated to terminate one, even when it was quite evident that it needed to be done. I was determined to scrutinize the patterns in my life, come to terms with my part in creating the situation, and to stop playing the victim.

Late one evening during meditation, I asked to know the truth about my relationships. I was not looking for the "textbook" version of the truth; I wanted to know the connection between my spiritual being, my emotions, and my beliefs. I wanted to know how they merged to manifest in all my relationships. I was looking for an epiphany!

That spring, I discovered the season of new beginnings, of rebirth, of growth, is also the season that restores our faith…if we let it. This is the season when we can learn that life, as we see it with our eyes, is not all there is to see. Sometimes we need to go

The 5 Phases Of Dating

deep, deep within ourselves to fully learn the meaning of "rebirth."

One night during that season, I fell asleep. When I awoke, my eyes would not open. My soaked pillow, my swollen eyes, and my runny nose clearly indicated that I had cried through the night. I forced my eyes open, washed my face, cleared my head, grabbed my journal, and began to recall my dream's messages. I went on a journey that night. Here is what I recorded:

Journey Through My Heart

It was so peaceful the way my heart answered all my questions. She held my hand and immediately I felt love-a love that expanded beyond anything I had ever known. Even though I knew I was about to relive all my past pain, I was not afraid. I felt safe.

I asked to know the source of my pain, the reasons why I had been treated so unfairly, and the reasons why I stayed in relationships that were not emotionally nurturing to me. I needed to know what I could do to create and receive the love that I really wanted.

With her holding my hand, we stepped over the broken shards of my heart, stopping at areas of darkness that materialized right before my eyes. I relived each relationship one by one, with portal-by-portal coming to light, not with the emotion attached to it, but with each question being answered.

She showed me how I had lost myself, my way, how

I loved each person more than I loved myself. She showed me how I gave away so much of myself, that once without that person, like an accident victim in physical therapy, I had to learn to walk again. I had to learn how to breathe again, alone and lonely. Each time I would promise myself that it would be different next time.

Each time it was different. The players were different and the pluses and minuses were different. I saw how each time I started out strong, but due to searching outside of myself for the love I so desperately needed and not putting myself first, I conceded. Though the relationships were different, the underlying lesson from each of them was always the same..."to thine own self be true."

Each time it started out as a great adventure but eventually turned onto a different path. Once I noticed the change in course, I felt that it was "not nice" to just bail out. I saw how my fear of failure kept me trying harder to receive and prove that I deserved what only I could give myself...unconditional love.

I saw and realized that I could not blame the other people in the relationships because one thing was for sure, they were true to themselves. Those who started out selfish, remained selfish. Those who were needy, remained needy. Those who were unable to commit, remained non-committal. It was I who had changed.

It was I who altered my life, so as not to cause the other person to be insecure. It was I who decided not to do those things that fed my spirit. It was I who overlooked consistent disrespectful acts-continuing to cry, beg, plead,

The 5 Phases Of Dating

and dramatize to have those things that should only come natural to me.

Each portal revealed a lesson, and then disappeared, leaving my heart a little lighter. My heart and I held hands and walked together through the pain, the disappointment, the fear of abandonment, the deceit from others and the deceit of myself. Neither of us uttered a single word, instead we communicated through our souls.

When it was over, we returned to the same place where the journey had begun. She looked lovingly into my eyes, opened her arms, and hugged me until I could feel the pain of the past dissolve away. She then released her grip on my soul, looked me in the eyes, and disappeared. I thought to myself...the future is up to me now. The past is not my destiny. I have the willpower and the strength to shape my life the way I want it to be.

This was a true awakening for me and the beginning of my return from the land of the scorned; it showed me the reality of myself. The more I asked to know, the more that was revealed to me. It was as though the Universe had turned me inside out and dissected my distorted memories one by one. The things that I learned about myself were not pretty. They were just as mean, conniving, spiteful, manipulative, degrading, vindictive, hateful, and abusive as I considered others to be. Having to face my own reality was extremely difficult. While most of my life I considered myself to be the **best** girlfriend ever, but I recognized that by consistently playing this role, I was also consistently neglecting my spirit, and for that I had paid a very high price.

These dark nights of my soul lasted for eighteen

months during which time I formed my philosophy, *The 5 Phases of Dating*™. I spent so much energy trying to avoid the pain of relating that my initial draft was devoid of emotion. You know, the "warm-n-fuzzies" that we all feel in the beginning? This system was sure to prevent the possibility of falling into the trap of the "warm-n-fuzzies" by offering a definite plan of "counter-attack" that would protect the heart. As I continued to walk around protected, stating upfront to suitors that I was living my life by *The 5 Phases*, amazing things started to happen.

Initially it began as a way to shield my heart, but by utilizing *The 5 Phases*, I managed to slow down long enough to see my dating situations with clarity. The result was an ability to see "what was" as compared to "what I wanted." I could see what was working for me and what was not, and in the process, I realized that I had achieved what once seemed impossible for me. I had completely shut down the emotional aspect of myself and found that I could be involved with an individual, truly enjoy their company, and yet not think twice about beginning a relationship. One suitor told me that my mannerisms and my stance on dating were like that of a man, which was the ability to be physical without becoming emotionally entangled. Of course, to me, that was the point. I felt that we women tend to fall heart first without allowing our head time to truly assess the situation. Therefore, the feelings had to go.

To some, it may have seemed cold-hearted, but at that time, it was what I needed to do in order to maintain my sense of self, while healing from my past. One thing that I could not be accused of doing was leading anyone on; I was very candid

The 5 Phases Of Dating

about my position on *The 5 Phases*. To avoid confusion and prevent anyone from feeling any sense of ownership of me, I made it clear that I was dating more than one person in various phases. Looking back, would I change anything? I would have to say no. Placing myself in the "5 Phases cocoon" allowed me the time I needed to nurture my spirit and heart into a brand-new way of communicating, thinking, and feeling.

I boldly stated in my columns, as well as to potential suitors at that time, that I would not begin a relationship for at least two years. (Just shows how arrogant we can be sometimes especially when we actually think that we have control over everything!) I had created and perfected my 3 Lists: *Must Haves, Can Compromise and Hell Naws*. During my *5 Phases Boot Camp*, I learned that I could shift items across lists if I deemed necessary as my experiences with each person were different. I also learned it was okay to do so. I learned more things about myself as each person served as a mirror for me, either revealing different parts of myself that I didn't know existed, or demonstrating parts that I thought I had conquered. This gave me the opportunity to stand still with each issue and not run from or deny it. I was in a state of readiness; I was ready to explore and heal, and by doing so, I moved closer and closer to truly knowing my *Purrfectly Authentic*™ self.

So why am I writing this book if I felt as though my initial involvement with *The 5 Phases* was totally one-sided? I am writing because I realized during this time that not every dating situation is a potential relationship, and that at times two people will cross each other's path because they have something to teach one another. The challenge is to slow down enough to recognize the lesson. That is what *The 5 Phases of Dating* is all about,

Anita M. Charlot

illustrating in each phase what to pay attention to, not only with the other person, but also within yourself. If you are looking for a book to confirm your greatness or to verify that every unfavorable dating situation is the direct result of the other person not understanding you, then perhaps this book will not satisfy your needs. If you want to hold on to your victim status, then you may want to put this book down now. If you are ready to look within, however, and see that most often these unfavorable situations occur because *you* do not understand *yourself,* then read on. Hopefully you will identify with what I learned in my own healing journey, and at its conclusion, you will find greater satisfaction within your relationships because you will have developed a better relationship with yourself.

While this book does not point fingers at the other person, it will open your eyes to the reality of your true self, shadow side and all. By answering the questions and doing the exercises presented, you will come to a new understanding about yourself and your patterns, with regard to not only dating, but also with regard to how these "epiphanies" spread across varied areas of your life.

INTRODUCTION

At one point in my life, I thought that my purpose in life was to feel and experience heartache, disappointment, shame, embarrassment, and low self-esteem so that I could help others heal from the very same things. That had to be the reason I experienced all the pain and BS that I did.

I didn't think that love, in the way that I wanted/needed to experience love, was possible for me. So, I learned everything I could about interpersonal relationships. I visited psychologists, psychotherapists, psychoanalysts, LCSWs, ministers, and first ladies. You name it, I went to them seeking clarity and understanding of what had happened in my love life and why I couldn't seem to get it right.

It wasn't until I went to see a metaphysician that things started to fall into place for me. I needed someone that would be able to not only see my mental or my spiritual, but also my energetic experiences. I also needed someone who would provide practical exercises and be able to connect with me like a loving "tell it like it is auntie." That is when I began recalling the fragmented pieces of my spirit, reclaiming my life, and truly learned how to date and relate from my truth. ***That*** is who I am for you!!!

If you're looking for a book to read and walk away with all the answers, this one isn't for you. If you are ready to do the following:

- put in the **work** to attract the dating and relationship situations that you want;
- want to know how to discern BS when it steps to you; and
- desire to develop the patience to not jump on top of and in the bed with the first thing that comes along that sounds good, smells good and makes your toes curl with a single touch

then *this* is the book for you.

Part therapeutic, part big sister, part "that auntie," and over twenty years in the game, if you apply what you read, do the work, and stay connected to your truth, while being honest about your own shortcomings, then you are guaranteed to view your dating and relationship experiences differently than you did before picking up this book.

Are you tired of repeating the same old patterns every time you date? Can you fight the need for immediate gratification? Would you like to go into your next relationship emotionally healthy and speaking from your *Purrfectly Authentic*™ voice? This book will first help you to identify your true wants, needs and desires; secondly, it will present a blueprint for you, while exploring *The 5 Phases*. If followed, this plan will help you clarify what is truly important to you and how to use this information to attract the man that is perfectly imperfect for you. While you are on this journey, I will also show you how to avoid some of the traps and the pitfalls grown-ass women tend to find themselves in during the search for that "perfect man."

The information that I share will be a culmination of over twenty years in the field of interpersonal relationships, specifically dating and relationship coaching. I will use real life

The 5 Phases Of Dating

examples of my own personal encounters, experiences of clients, friends, family members and women that I have coached in some of my workshops. While this book will present a guide for you to pursue your path of personal growth and development, it cannot possibly answer every question or resolve every problem. I wrote this book to provide information and insight; used wisely it will open your mind and help you work through your own personal situations.

For some, it may be an arduous process, as I will bypass the lies that you have been told, as well as those you have been telling yourself, and go straight for the secrets we pray are never found out, the insecurities and fears that we do not want others to see.

I like to consider myself not only a coach, but also a relationship architect. Relationships don't just happen. You must work at them and keep building on them, sort of like building a house.

As a result, each of *The 5 Phases* has a corresponding home-building analogy. The breakdown of *The 5 Phases* is as follows:

Phases	Dating and Relationships	Building a Home
I	Friendship	Locating the Desired Neighborhood
II	Dating: Non-Committed	Surveying the Landscape
III	Dating: Committed Relationship	Laying the Foundation
IV	Engagement	Building the House
V	Marriage	Maintaining the Home and Adding on Rooms

Now let's take a closer look at how these are connected. To be successful in **any** dating or relationship situation, you must first take the time to lay your **own** foundation. It does not matter if you are currently on sabbatical from the dating scene, actively dating, in a committed relationship or married, you will benefit from doing the introspective exercises in the first chapter. Continue through the remaining chapters for insight into the ways in which we as grown-ass women either lose ourselves, or we become so protective of ourselves that we stand in the way of the love that we say we **really** want. If you stay open and are honest with yourself, then you are sure to catch a glimpse or two of your own behaviors in several sections (maybe all of them), and I'm certain that you will enjoy several, "Aha!" moments in the process.

Please understand that these assignments will require great commitment from you and the willingness to look **your** truth directly in the eye, whether you consider the reflection to be something that you can be proud of or not. While it may be difficult, we will take this journey together.

You may experience times when you cannot put the book down, and then again, there may be times when you will not only put it down, but you will also vow never to pick it up again! That is a normal reaction to this type of self-exploration. If the assignments and the introspective questions do not affect you (positively or negatively), then quite possibly you may not be looking deep enough, or perhaps you are not being truthful with yourself. Only you know the answers within you; this is your personal journey to become acquainted with the truth of who you have been so that you can make any adjustments as needed. Please

The 5 Phases Of Dating

be gentle with yourself, understanding, loving, and especially forgiving. This book is not about pointing out your faults, but more so for providing you with an "inside view" into the differences in what you say you want and what you currently attract based on your hidden behaviors.

As you run into these challenging moments, promise yourself that you are going to see it through to the end. If it helps, read the book first cover-to-cover for completion, then read it again for true interaction and comprehension. You will gain knowledge by just reading the book, but the real transformation happens when you fully engage in the exercises, do the work, and "grow through" those things that will set you on the path to attracting and maintaining the love you've always wanted.

You are bound to come across the recognition that all your failed relationships are not the fault of the other person, and several were a result of your own behavior and emotional evolution. When you recognize this, cut yourself some slack realizing that once you become aware of your behavior patterns, you have the choice whether to change them or not. It is up to you! If you choose not to change, then be willing to accept yourself **completely** for who you are and continue to move forward learning how to attract the man that will accept you for who you **really** are.

Each individual phase is written to help you identify the areas in which you are not being true to yourself and to reveal the patterns in your life that block your ability to experience happiness in your relationships. It will also identify the countless subconscious choices that we make that undermine our true desires and intentions. Upon completing your journey, consider how it has helped you; perhaps you know someone who would appreciate the opportunity to take it as well. I would love to hear from you, and will personally respond to every email. Here is my email address anita@anitacharlot.com. Be sure to put **#5phases** in the subject line.

The more aware we are of the hidden causes behind the demise of our relationships, the better prepared we are to make the adjustments necessary and to obtain the love that we so desire and deserve. Whether that adjustment is a major life change or simply recognition of who you really are inside, in these pages you will learn the spirit of the man that is perfectly imperfect for you and how to identify those specific traits in the men that cross your path.

Prepare to get your practice dates in. Date for the enjoyment of dating and acquire the patience required to make better decisions when it comes to opening your heart. Every man you date is not entitled to all of you right away. I will teach you how to manage this as well.

If you have ever been on a call with me, a client of mine, a guest on a radio show, or a student of mine, you know I give homework. It's one thing for you to hear or read the information, but it's another thing for you to do the work.

Here is a list of tools that you will need to assist you on this introspective journey:
- A journal to record your answers, thoughts, dreams, questions, etc.;
- An open mind and a willingness to see yourself as you **really** are;
- A box of tissue for those moments in which you are reliving a past hurt or pain, in order to let it go; and
- The link to schedule a 20 Minute Complimentary

The 5 Phases Of Dating

Discovery Session should you want to explore personalized coaching packages. Just go to bit.ly/booktimewithanita

My Dating and Relationship History

The following information is not something that I have readily shared with the masses, however, I feel it's important for you to understand what my relationship history has been so that you can see that with or without certain letters behind my name, I have a PhD in dating and relationships. After years of searching, wanting, desiring certain qualities and characteristics of the male/female relationship, I reasoned that what I really wanted did not exist. A good friend introduced me to a different way of relating in relationships: a relationship without a man. After two children, a failed marriage, and countless affectionless relationships, I figured since I could not get the unconditional acceptance, affection, nurturing, respect, caring, emotional connection, and attachment that I longed for in a relationship with a man, why not try a relationship with a woman? Well, this "test" period lasted for over twelve years.

How could I go wrong? Certainly, a woman would have the inside track on how to make another woman happy, right? Would she not know how to make her female partner feel special, loved, cherished, and adored? She would neither play the same mind games, nor have the same infidelity issues as men, correct? She would not mentally, physically, or emotionally abuse the woman that she loved, would she? I thought I knew the answers to these ever-present, relationship-bound questions because after all, we were cut from the same cloth?

Society is a lot more accepting of same-gender relationships than they were twenty years ago. However, my own religious upbringing forced me into hiding. I felt that God and the world would punish me if I disclosed my secret, a secret that I had been taught was a sin. I wrestled with this decision for years. In counseling I tried to figure out where this was all coming from. How was it so easy for me to "flip the script"? All of these things went through my mind, but the need or desire for a fulfilling relationship was not going to allow me to just ignore it.

I cannot speak for all women, or men for that matter, since everyone's personal experience is different. However, I felt compelled to develop a mechanism for myself and countless other women in my position to freely express themselves and seek solace and comfort when needed. Ultimately, I created the company Purrfect Harmony Unlimited, Inc. This was my contribution to honor lesbian and bisexual mothers, to help women, like me, who struggled to feel accepted, and to let them know that they were not alone. During this time, I began coaching many women and felt that I could safely speak on their behalf. I was determined to be the voice for other women like myself; we were going to be heard!

Well, to my surprise, the things that I thought would **not** take place in a lesbian relationship **did**...and then some. Only this time there were a lot more devastating, emotional, and drama-filled encounters than a heterosexual relationship because in my heart I had expected, even sometimes justified that behavior from men.

I went into the LGBTQ community believing that the

The 5 Phases Of Dating

grass would be greener and, to my huge disappointment, found that it was not. The likelihood of infidelity is much greater; trust is a major issue; and not knowing whether your girlfriend's friend is really her friend or a "love interest" can drive you mad! Whereas, in a heterosexual relationship, when your boyfriend/husband says that he is going to "hang out with his friends," you assume that he is doing just that.

What I discovered throughout this period was that there are many facets to alternative lifestyles; I felt like an onion, peeling back the layers. The unwritten code of ethics as it relates to heterosexual relationships can be completely different in the alternative lifestyle arena depending upon whom you are dating, their family, relationship history, whether they have dated men before, their nationality, and social status. One would think that neither racism, nor prejudice would exist because society already considered us a sub-class. My assumption was that we would embrace each other and at least have camaraderie amongst our own. This was **not** the case, and therefore, another awakening revelation.

The code of ethics regarding mutual respect and respect for the concept of commitment is also different. Behaviors that would not be acceptable in the heterosexual community appear to be taken lightly in the LGBTQ community. A prime example is allowing people that have an intimate interest in you to be a part of your life and ultimately causing dissention in your relationship. Also, allowing the person that you are dating to move into your home within the first month, walking away from a relationship or a living arrangement and leaving the other person stuck with all of the financial responsibility. You name it...it existed.

Abuse is not an isolated problem only common to heterosexual relationships; women experience abuse in LGBTQ relationships as well. Visible scars are not the only proof of violence in a relationship. In other words, *you don't have to hit me to hurt me.* While the emotional connection may be greater between two women than it is between a man and a woman, the betrayal of that connection was even more devastating. Women lied. They cheated. They slept around. They physically, mentally, and emotionally abused their female partners. I was shocked! I have experienced these situations personally, along with many of the women I coached. Many of us who have walked away from the heterosexual community in search of that ultimate connection with a woman were disappointed to find it was the "same shit," just a different gender.

Once I sat down and looked at the differences and the similarities between the two, I realized and now subscribe a different philosophy. While there are many differences between men and women, such as physical intimacy, common interests, menstrual cycles, and birthing children, **queer relationships face the same challenges as heterosexual ones**. It is not the gender of the person, but rather his or her spirit that nurtures your soul, and subsequently the relationship. Women are just as capable of abuse and infidelity as men. Having the same anatomical structure doesn't make another woman more capable or even willing to have the same ideology about the "perfect relationship" as you do.

So where did I end up after my research period? On which side of the fence did I land? How would I classify myself? These are good questions. I would have to say that I am pansexual. There were certain parts that I enjoyed about being in a relationship with a woman, and there were aspects that I

The 5 Phases Of Dating

enjoyed about being in a relationship with a man. However, the most important thing that I have learned is to first have a relationship with **myself** and not settle for anything less than what I deserve regardless of my sexual orientation.

What qualifies me to speak to you about relationships? Simply put, I experienced relationships from both a heterosexual and queer point of view. I have lived on both sides of the fence. I have lived through the trials and tribulations of both situations. As a result, I created The 5 Phases of Dating series to speak to the spirit of the person you are dating. For simplicity sake, I will describe relationships in this book in terms of male or female; however, feel free to change the pronouns as you see fit. Don't get lost in labels. Focus on the message.

It is my prediction that someone looking for information on dating and wanting to look at it from a new perspective will find value in the information presented here. I have taken over twenty-five years of personal experience, combined with that of my clients and workshop attendees, and created my philosophy on how to view the dating world from a more authentic perspective.

My quest for the truth led me through many life-altering phases. I experienced several career changes, various relationships both intimate and friendships, different religious paths and many dark nights of the soul. Sometimes I felt like I would never find the love I wanted and I found myself knocking on death's door twice trying to escape the pain. Fortunately, once I began to get in touch and identify with the truth of who I was and learned to love myself unconditionally, things began to positively change for me.

Authentic in what way you may ask? By helping you

embrace your authentic self so that your dating situations will be more in line and in tune with who you really are, not who you thought yourself to be. We will do this by preparing you for the reality of dating by immersing you in thought-provoking, yet necessary introspective exercises that will break up your former patterns of communication and the way you previously related to others in prior relationships. Grab your journals and let's get ready to see yourself as the beautiful, however complex woman that you are!

Dedication of Your Purrfectly Authentic™ Journal (Paj)

Before we go any further, I would like for you to take a moment and write a dedication for your journal. First, find a quiet space to eliminate external distractions and other noises. You may want to play some soft music, run a hot bubble bath, grab a glass of wine, a cup of coffee or tea, light a candle, etc. Do whatever you need to do to get into in a relaxed mood. Once your atmosphere is conducive to relaxation and concentration, take a few deep breaths. Now, I would like to suggest that you write a *letter of dedication* to yourself on the very first page(s).

In this letter:
- Set the intention for what you want to accomplish by reading this book.
- List the information/insight that you are looking forward to obtaining from these pages.
- Determine what you want to walk away with.

The 5 Phases Of Dating

Having a good idea of what you want to accomplish will provide a signal to your spirit to tune into those situations. This will significantly increase the possibility of those issues being brought into your awareness. Recognize that you will come across some information that seems irrelevant to you or where you are in your quest. My suggestion is that you take what you need from what is revealed and leave the rest; hence, you never know when that particular lesson may cross your path in the future.

Also, give yourself credit for taking the time to get in touch with your truth and your authentic self. Acknowledge yourself as someone who deserves more than what you have experienced. See yourself as someone who deserves all the love that you can handle, as well as all of the intimacy that you want. Finally, understand that you **can** have it. It's yours for the taking! You just need to know what your blocks have been, and then take the time to heal from them. Once you remember who you are and what your true needs are, then you'll realize you're worthy **just because** you are alive! Eventually, you'll learn how to recognize the spirit of the person that is perfectly imperfect for you.

Once you begin to recognize, acknowledge, and completely accept yourself, and as you become crystal clear about your needs, wants, and desires, you will begin to attract those very things into your life. No matter what your spiritual background is, once you see it, you can achieve it. But you must be able to see it *clearly* first!

At the end of your dedication letter, I would like for you to place this pledge:

This or something better now manifests for me, in totally satisfying and harmonious ways, for the good of all concerned.
You can end this statement by using *Amen, And So It Is, And So Mote It Be;* it totally depends on your personal preference.

Once completed, then sign and date it. It doesn't matter if it takes you two months to complete the exercises in this book, or two years to fill up your journal. Just know that embarking upon this journey is a very courageous thing, and in case no one else tells you...I'M PROUD OF YOU!!!

Now, let's get started by building the most important relationship you will ever have, the relationship with yourself!!! You are so worth it!

PART 1: INTERNAL GROUNDWORK: GETTING IN TOUCH WITH YOUR PURRFECTLY AUTHENTIC™ SELF

Anita M. Charlot

DEFINING YOUR PURRFECTLY AUTHENTIC™ RELATIONSHIP

On the next page of your PAJ, I would like for you to write at the top: *A day in the life of my Purrfectly Authentic Relationship.* Then, on the lines that follow, describe what that day would look like. Make sure you write about it in the present tense and select a day of the week that is most important to you. It could be a work day or a weekend. Begin writing about your perfect day from the time you wake up until the time you go to bed.

The important thing here is to begin to get in touch with the "feeling" of being in this relationship. How do you want to be treated? How do you want to be talked to? How would you want your mate to interact with you? Describe the day doing things that you love to do, the things that speak directly to your heart. Don't worry about being selfish. This is your story and you are crafting **your** perfect day…so make it perfect!

Describe as best as possible:
- What it would feel like.
- What he would sound like when he speaks to you.
- What small things did you wish your previous mates would have done for you or to you?
- How would he treat you?

- How would you respond to him?
- How do you want to feel when you are around him?

Be as specific as you can. Really think about this description. Don't hold anything back. This is *a day in the life of your perfectly authentic* relationship and no one has to read what it is you **really** want unless you share it with them, so let go. You have my permission to be as specific as you want to be.

PURRFECTLY AUTHENTIC VOCABULARY

Each time I begin with a new client, one of our first exercises is learning all about the *Purrfectly Authentic™ Vocabulary*. The client's first reaction is usually frustration and the feeling that they are being treated as though they are in grade school. Once I see that all too familiar look on her face, I always ask, "Do you see something wrong with the homework assignment that you have just been given? If so, please be honest with me."

They usually reply, "I feel as though you are insulting my intelligence by asking me to do definitions. This isn't quite what I expected you to ask me to do. I thought this was about finding out who I really am deep down inside, not an English class." I love the responses. Just the facial expressions alone in response to the homework assignment lets me know how rewarding this will be for them. I assure them, just as I'm assuring you, that although this seems like an English assignment, you'll be surprised at the level of difficulty you might have in defining the terms you typically throw around so freely.

Exercise

Now, it's your turn. I want you to extract from your *Purrfectly Authentic* relationship the words that you used to describe the characteristics of your *Purrfectly Authentic* mate. In your journal, place one word at the top of each of the following pages. I suggest you list only one characteristic per page; however, I want you to write it twice: once on the very top line and again in the middle of the page.

At the top of the page I want you to define what you feel that characteristic means. For example:

I want my mate to be **honest. Honesty** *to me means...*
Keep in mind that you cannot use any form of the actual word in your definition. You cannot define honesty as "being completely honest with me...or communicating with me honestly, etc." You have to break down what you feel honesty means. I will give you an example from one of my clients:
Honest: Honesty to me means someone always telling me the truth; being open about their feelings; telling me exactly what's on their mind.

Now I want you to do the same thing. Define each characteristic in as much detail as you can. Be very specific. Be sure that you are defining the actual characteristic that

The 5 Phases Of Dating

you listed. Try to stick to the word that you started with and not veer off into something else. This is easier said than done. Let me show you:

Remember the definition of my client...
Honest: Honesty to me means always telling me the truth; being open about their feelings; telling me exactly what's on their mind.

Hey, this sounds like something we all want, right? Well I have a surprise for you...this definition was not the definition that she ended up with. This definition includes several characteristics. Honesty, according to her definition, not only includes being honest, but it also includes something else that is very important to her...an open line of communication. Could you see that by reading her definition the first time? Did you feel as though it was Purrfect just the way it was? That it was complete?

This is where we make our mistake. When we use common terms that are used every day and we do not take the time to *really* determine how those terms actually fit into our lives-how we in our *Purrfectly Authentic* moments actually feel about these terms deep down-we run the risk of not getting what we want because we are not *clear* as to what we want.

Stop reading here. Take all the time you need to complete your assignment. Only after you have listed and defined all the characteristics you seek in your Purrfectly Authentic mate should you return to the book. Don't worry! You're not being graded. So don't rush. Take your time. After all, your work here will lay the groundwork for the rest of your life. Give yourself all the time you need! I'll wait for you.
Ready?

Now, what I want you to do is to go back over each and every page of characteristics you defined. Go to the middle of the page, review the definition as you stated it at the top of the page, and dissect it. Determine whether within that particular definition you are also defining another characteristic that you want. If so, rewrite the original definition to address only the characteristic on that page, and turn to a new page and write the new desired characteristic that you just uncovered.

The new characteristic should be dissected just as thoroughly as the original. You want to keep breaking these definitions down until you get to the core of what's true for you. No matter how shallow, how superficial, or how silly you think you sound, **be** totally clear about what you want in a relationship. The whole point here is to define as clearly as possible those things which you feel are necessary to have the relationship that you want.

Let me share an exchange with a client. The word she chose was **honest**:

Client: I want my Purrfectly Authentic mate to be honest.
Me: Okay, define honest.
Client: I don't know...um...honest.
Me: How does honest feel? When you think of honest what comes to mind?
Client: Well, I want them to always tell me how they feel. If something is wrong, I want them to tell me. If they are sad, I want them to tell me that too. I don't want to have to guess when it comes to what they are feeling.
Me: Listening to your definition, it sounds to me as though you are describing your *Purrfectly Authentic* mate being able to

The 5 Phases Of Dating

openly communicate their feelings with you and be completely honest while doing so. Would you agree?
Client: Well, I guess so. I never really broke it down like that before.
Me: If you were to tell someone that you wanted honesty and they gave you what they considered to be their definition of honesty, do you see how this would lead you into making that same statement of "No one understands me?"
Client: I guess it would be confusing, especially if I was saying one thing, but I really meant something else.
Me: Can you see how not clearly defining the ***feeling*** behind the character traits of this *Purrfectly Authentic* person can leave a lot of room for misunderstanding and for not actually getting what you want?
Client: Yes, I can. And I thought this exercise had no value. Now I'm going to have to take some time to really sit and think about these definitions.

Take these additional thoughts and questions into consideration when defining your terms:
- Do not use the word in the definition.
- What does this trait feel like?
- How would a person show you this trait in your relationship with him or her?

The average person usually has no patience for this exercise. We live in a society of getting everything we want and fast as we can get it. It pays to do your homework, not only for yourself, but also for the potential relationship as well. The more you know about yourself and the other person upfront, the better choice you can make as to whether or not to enter into that relationship.

Anita M. Charlot

YOUR THREE LISTS: MUST HAVES, CAN COMPROMISE ONS, AND HELL NAWS!

Your next assignment is to complete your three lists. Now that you have fully described the character traits that you want in a mate, it's time to place them in their proper categories. As we all know, you will never find one person who will exemplify each and every single trait that you want them to have, so the idea here is to determine the order of importance of the listed traits, as well as, others that will come to mind once you begin this particular exercise.

The three lists that you will be creating are as follows:

I. Your Must Haves
II. Your Can Compromise Ons
III. Your Hell Naws!

Each one of these lists is very important. Grab your journal. Start with a fresh sheet of paper, and on the top of each new sheet write the title of each list. Do not write on the back of either page as you will be surprised by how many things you add to these individual lists. Once you have the title listed at the top, go back through your character traits. Place each character trait on the appropriate page. Be sure to add any additional thoughts or ideas that might come to mind when creating these three lists, no matter how silly or

The 5 Phases Of Dating

inconsequential they may seem at the time. The idea here is to flush it *all* out. We will determine what to keep and what not to keep later (for your BONUS 3-Lists Mini-Course, go to bit.ly/3listsfree).

For example, I had five **Must Haves** on my list. I had written: (1) *Must have the majority of their original teeth in their mouth* (hey, the majority of America has had some form of dental work); (2) *must have hair on their head* (okay, this applied to women only); (3) *must have a belief in a higher power;* (4) *must be able to speak clearly;* (5) *must have a life outside of me.* This is no joke. On my **Can Compromise Ons** list, I had written that *I am flexible or can compromise on these things: height, weight, career choice,* and *level of spirituality.* And on my **Hell Naws!** list, I had things like, *smoking, cheating, lying, stealing, drug habits,* and *offensive body odor.*

I'm sure you get the point.

You can get as crazy as you want with this. It is for your eyes only! I must admit, though, going over these lists with my clients has shown me that I am not the only person with certain levels of expectation in certain areas. It's always fun to hear the reasons behind why they chose specific criteria. During our time of going over the assignment, it is very common for women to feel embarrassed at some of the things they place on their lists.

By the time we are done analyzing and reviewing the three lists, they begin to understand that it is okay for them to like what they like and dislike what they dislike at this point in their lives. They eventually realize these lists are not permanent. They possess the ability at any time to shift items across lists as they see fit. You never know. What is an annoyance today might be a soothing element tomorrow. Your lists should change, grow, and evolve through a metamorphosis, just as you will.

WAIT...WHAT? I THOUGHT WE WERE IN A RELATIONSHIP?!?!

So, what is this dating and relationship thing? How do you know when you are in which phase? Hang tight. I'm getting there.

The introductory phase begins the moment you meet a person and feel that they are someone you would like to get to know better. During this phase, when you are open to the possibilities of dating, you should not behave as though you are desperate. I can say with complete confidence that one of your friends, family members, or maybe even you have acted out of desperation at one point or another. We all do, until we learn how to behave differently.

You know the desperate woman type. You've seen her before. She's the one always talking about having been the victim, bragging about how she treated her exes, or how she went out of her way to be accommodating and being overly nice. Better yet, sometimes she even borders on stalking. She constantly calls the man who has shown very little interest in her even after she hasn't heard from him in over a week. She might

The 5 Phases Of Dating

call him with this excuse, "I just wanted to make sure that you were okay. Call me!" She goes out of her way to try and prove to her love interest at the time that she is someone that he should be interested in. If this is you or anyone you know, you need to realize that a man can spot desperation a mile away. He may hook up with you in the short term, already knowing within himself that you will never be long-term material. But the desperate woman will not see this for what it is. She will make up an excuse for him: *he's busy, he worked late, he doesn't like to use his phone.*

For those who are tired of the dating scene or of being alone, there seems to be a natural tendency to start immediately thinking of that new person in terms of a potential relationship. This can be particularly troublesome. When you are first attracted to someone, there is always a spark, the "warm-n-fuzzies" as I like to call it. These "warm-n-fuzzies" feel so good; they constantly make us tingle, and as a result, we cannot stop thinking about this person and all the possibilities. This infatuation may lead to **premature speculation** about a future with this new person. For instance, it could be May, but we are already thinking about what to buy them for Christmas.

Sometimes when someone has been without a relationship for a long time, they make the mistake of giving too much information (TMI). These pursuers share too much too early, especially things that are not appropriate so soon in a developing relationship. They begin to speak in what Carolyn Myss calls "woundology," (1996). They play the victim. They share the details of past relationships, how they suffered great injustice and how they tried consistently to please an ungrateful partner. You may recognize this pattern since many of us have done it at one time or another in our lives.

I also noticed during this quest for a new relationship, some people approach the new prospect as though they were applying for a job. They dress the part, say all the right things, have their interview answers memorized, and put their best foot forward in hopes of landing the "job." However, please be advised that there is an unspoken 3-6-9 rule that most dating relationships follow. You can't always judge a book by its cover.

THE 3-6-9 RULE

Each person is usually on his or her best behavior during the first three months of a courtship. They appear totally accepting; nothing seems to annoy them. They allow you to have control over the remote, let you decide where to have dinner or what movie to see, and agree to attend all your social gatherings. They may shower you with affection, return your calls and/or texts immediately, and they do not need a special occasion to send flowers, cards, or little gifts. If you do not like to do certain chores, then it's perfectly okay because it just happens to be something they don't mind doing. And if your interaction/relationship has become physical, then you will find that you cannot get enough of each other.

This is often referred to as the "honeymoon phase."

Here is the trap: the heat of the "honeymoon" fire slows to a simmer beginning around month four. During the next three months, the 3-6-month phase, things begin to change. Physical intimacy decreases. Flowers, cards and gifts become history. It takes longer to return texts/phone calls. You become

The 5 Phases Of Dating

more comfortable with the other person.

Picking a movie or maintaining control over the remote becomes more challenging. Little irritations begin to creep up, and your eyebrow raises as you notice subtle changes in the person's behavior or moods; however, most people are afraid to speak up for fear of rocking the boat. Most don't want to lose the "warm-n-fuzzies" by appearing to be a complainer so soon in the "relationship." You may be thinking that all relationships go through some difficulties, so you decide to ride the wave and see where it goes.

The 6-9-month phase brings an awareness of even more changes. You notice that this person is now vying for more independence and space, claiming to feel smothered, even though you assumed that you had created a "relationship." You back off because you do not want to scare them away; the "warm-n-fuzzies" are gone and you now second-guess yourself and the other person. You are wondering where you went wrong and/or what you did to cause the other person to change.

At this point, you might compare this feeling with past relationships and realize that this is exactly when things started going wrong in the last one, and you may even begin to think, "This is how Shawna acted!" or "John did this very same thing!" or "Rachel behaved in this same fashion, and we never recuperated from it." It's easy to take all the blame and to begin to question yourself. Did you cook the right foods? Did you perform well enough in bed? Does the other person still find you attractive? This is common. You might even say things like, "Am I being silly? Could it just be me and my insecurities that are creeping up again? Why does this always happen to me? My relationships usually don't last past 7-9 months?"

> Do not misconstrue this revelation as there is nothing wrong with introspection; however, the objective of *The 5 Phases* is to help you identify your patterns before getting into a dating relationship.

The next thing you know, the "relationship" is over. I've placed relationship in quotes because usually there has been no formal communication regarding the nature of your interaction. Two people meet. They start spending a lot of time together, and then they make assumptions based on their activities. They have unspoken expectations of the other person. They never sit down to discuss what they are doing. They just do it. They do not take time to figure out if they speak the same relationship language. Suddenly, when one person gets tired, they just stop doing it, whatever *it* was that they were doing.

How do you stop this nonsense? What could you do to make better choices? How could you determine if you and a potential dating partner are compatible before you spend a lot of time and emotional energy? Well, that is where *The 5 Phases* will come in handy, but first, here is another journal exercise (yeah, I know):

Exercise:
In your journal, answer these questions

- What is a relationship?
- What should it feel like? What should it look like?

The 5 Phases Of Dating

- What do you want in your quest to share your life with another person?
- What is currently missing in your life?
- Are you behaving desperate. If so, why?
- What gap are you trying to fill?
- What relationship from your past are we trying to heal: family, friendship, or past relationship?

Once you have a good idea of what these terms and concepts mean to you at this time, we will go on to examine *The 5 Phases of Dating*. I guarantee by the time you are done with this book, and you look back to review these questions, you will see how much your perception has changed and how much you have grown.

As a reminder, here is the breakdown of *The 5 Phases of Dating* again:

I. Friendship – Locating the Desired Neighborhood
II. Dating (Non-committed) – Surveying the Landscape
III. Committed Relationship – Laying the Foundation
IV. Engagement – Building the House
V. Marriage – Maintaining the Home and Adding Additions

We will relate the process of dating to that of building a house, which explains the analogies above. First, you must take the time to lay your **own** foundation. It does not matter if you are currently on sabbatical from the dating scene, actively dating someone (or several some ones), in a committed relationship, or married. You will still benefit from doing the introspective exercises in the first chapter. Those who are willing to look closely at how they lose sight of themselves when dating by choosing to continue this path of self-exploration will identify with many, if not all, of the sections of this book. There are sure to be many "aha!" moments along the way. Understand that these assignments will require great commitment from you and the willingness to look **your** truth directly in the eye. There will be moments of great pride and other moments of deep shame, guilt, and regret. Therefore, it will not always be an easy task. Your rate of success will be measured by how deep down you are willing to travel to come face-to-face with your emotions. Remember, you are not alone. We are taking this journey together.

Ready? Let's begin!

PART 2: THE 5 PHASES OF DATING

Anita M. Charlot

PHASE I: FRIENDSHIP - LOCATING THE DESIRED NEIGHBORHOOD

Proposed Timeline

The time you spend in each Phase is always a matter of personal choice; however, I will make a few suggestions. For the initial friendship phase, I suggest you allow yourself at least three months to get to know this person without any physical interaction, including hand holding or kissing. For some, this will sound extreme, but believe it or not, you will be grateful for it later. Physical contact tends to cloud your judgment by placing you in the realm of the "warm-n-fuzzies" versus reality. These are the things that need to be considered during Phase I.

What You See Is What You Get

Is this person tall enough? Is he or she short enough? What is his or her personal style? I know these questions might seem superficial, but whether you want to admit it or not, you are consciously or subconsciously looking at these very qualities. Is there enough there to please the eye? If not, you will not be interested in getting to know this person any further, so be realistic. Would you want to go into a dating situation feeling as though you were not completely free to be who you are? No! So be cautious about making statements such as, "They are a diamond in the rough. All they need is a woman like me, an updated wardrobe, to stop swearing, smoking, or eating with their mouth open." Or, "They're nice. Just let me get them out of those bolero jackets and crocheted ties, and they'll be good to go!" (Don't laugh. I am describing my ex-husband here). Anyway, I've made my point. If you don't like their style in the beginning, then you have no right to try to make them change. The person may be open to it and even ask for your guidance; however, you run the risk of being resented for it later. Have a clear idea of what you want and know that it is out there somewhere. As soon as you stop focusing on that *something* and begin focusing on yourself, you will attract that which you desire.

Evaluation Time!

Okay, now the fun begins...

This is the time to start looking at how the person measures up against your three lists. The lists are not to be used literally; however, they should be used as a guide to determine whether this person is even near what you are looking for. What is great about this time is that even if you determine that they did not make the "cut," you will at least have made a connection with someone that could turn out to be a future friend.

Where Are They Now?

Are they married, currently dating, in a committed relationship, recently separated, divorced, or in a complicated situation? Should this matter? Of course, it should. Regardless of what they tell you, no recently separated person has had the opportunity to work through their feelings from that relationship. There is almost always a period of grieving that needs to occur, as well as time for introspection, whether they recognize it or not. To get involved with someone that is just out of a relationship means that you will be the rebound person. No matter what they tell you, you **will** play this role.

There is an old saying regarding this situation: "The fastest way to get over someone is to begin dating someone else." While this may take our mind off the former relationship, in the grand scheme of things, this approach is not the best for starting a new relationship. Starting a new relationship before allowing yourself the opportunity of grieving the previous one exposes you to the risk of being taken advantage of or unfortunately, *your* taking advantage of someone else.

The time after a relationship ends should be spent looking at **you** through your previous relationships and actions. This is the time to study the pros and cons, to think about the lessons learned, and to consider the benefits of those experiences. Ask yourself what you could have done differently. Did you value yourself and/or your partner? What sacrifices did you make that culminated in going against who you are on the inside? Did you take enough time to get to know the person in the beginning before committing to them? What would you do differently next time? Did you become intimate too soon? Is there anything that you recognized as a recurring pattern in all your relationships?

There are many things to consider, and if you realize that you are attracted to someone fresh out of a relationship, please know that you will be the rebound person. As the rebound person, you will endure incessant talk about their previous relationship, about how the other person did not appreciate them. You will be the therapist in their grieving process, and you will get a distorted view of what the reality of that relationship was. One reason will be that the person is most likely operating in victim mode, and they want so much for you to like them and see them as a good catch that they will exaggerate things to make themselves look like the better person. It's not that they are bad, but rather, this is all part of their healing. On the other hand, some individuals in this situation can also be very grateful for the attention, and therefore, appear very giving. They give you their wallet, all their free time, the world even, and yet they are not free to give their heart because they have not yet healed from the pain associated with ending their last relationship. After a while, you will notice that they begin to distance themselves, leaving you confused, resentful, second-guessing, and questioning yourself, when what you should be focusing on is loving and respecting yourself enough not to place yourself in that position.

This does not mean that you cannot socialize or hang out with anyone newly out of a relationship. Just be aware of their emotional fragility. If you are in the market for another platonic friend or maintenance partner (we will discuss this in detail during Phase 2), then okay, but if you are truly interested in a potential dating partner, then recognize that this person is not going to be able to give you all their attention or heart since their ex still resides there.

Discussion of *The 5 Phases* Of Dating

I would love to know that you are selecting this book for your book clubs or setting up café dates to discuss *The 5 Phases of Dating* with your potential mates, but I know that it is merely my recurring dream. When I learned something new that was helpful to me, I had the tendency to sing like a canary and act like a born-again Christian, if you will, singing praises and sharing my story with anyone that would listen. It took me years and several hard lessons to learn that some things are meant for individuals to learn in their own time and in their own private space.

Gaining knowledge is a wonderful thing. Talking incessantly about it is not. How many times have you resented your friend for talking about their new love interest all the time? You look at the caller ID, see who it is, and then let it go to voicemail. You avoid spending time with them until the first three months are over because we all know things usually begin to mellow around this time. If you begin singing the praises of the *The 5 Phases of Dating* with your potential dating options, you will make them run as fast as possible in the other direction. Trust me. I have tested and proven this theory.

What I quickly learned was that, even though I felt this would be a book to change how many would view the dating ritual, I found it was not something that everyone wanted to experience. Therefore, I say to you now, don't force the issue! If you want to discuss the book and its concepts, then keep it with you when meeting someone for lunch or coffee, or leave it out in clear view in your home, but allow the other person to bring it to your attention. This way they will not feel pressured or uneasy when discussing it.

I've heard a whole range of comments while getting input about *The 5 Phases*:

- No one is going to follow that.

The 5 Phases Of Dating

- That may work for women, but there isn't a brother alive that will slow things down that much.
- Good luck with that! I hope it works out for you.
- You are completely crazy for thinking people would buy this book, much less practice the concepts.

Now if this was the reaction I received just by talking about writing it, imagine the reaction you would receive by promoting and highlighting it to your potential mate about the value of *The 5 Phases*, much less taking the concepts seriously. This reminds me of a quote: "Those that know, don't tell and those that don't know, talk too damn much!" I am sure that I have probably changed the words to fit my personality, but the point is the same. Do not talk about it; act on it. We get so caught up trying to impress others with our knowledge of newly learned concepts that we spend more time talking about them than practicing them.

I don't expect you to buy into everything I say, nor do I advise you to. All I ask is that you take the time to read the entire book and do your best to apply some of the concepts. Test the waters a bit. Shape and mold the exercises to fit your life, no matter your sexual preference. Then, if you want to talk about the book, talk about the personal growth that you experienced because of having read it. Please understand that everyone is not ready to embrace the truth about themselves, and it is next to impossible to force feed anyone before their time. Just take care of you first and the rest will follow.

Once you find that your potential mate is open to discussing *The 5 Phases*, you might find it interesting to ask their opinion about dating rituals, to understand whether they have even given it serious thought. Engage in dialogue. Ask a few preliminary questions and compare definitions. By doing so, you will begin to understand where this person is on their relationship journey.

Here are a few questions for you to break the ice:
What do you think about the dating ritual?
Do you think dating is overrated?

- What are your thoughts about the different stages of dating?
- Do you see a difference in the different stages of dating, and if so, what would you consider those to be?
- How would you define the difference between dating and hanging out?
- How would you know when you have moved from the hanging out phase to the actual dating phase?

These are only a sample, but they will assist you in determining whether this is someone you would want to get to know better. Notice that I did not ask any of the standard questions like, *What type of person are you looking for? What do you want in a mate?* or *What qualities in a partner would turn you on?* These are superficial and not important in the beginning. You want to know if you speak the same dating lingo. If you do not speak the same language from the very beginning, communication later will only become increasingly difficult.

It does not hurt to ask these types of questions. They are simple, yet informative, and they will help you understand the other person. We tend to want to jump in feet first when we hear a comment or philosophical statement that we agree with,

The 5 Phases Of Dating

especially when we have something in common. **Don't do it!** Learn to listen and hear what they are saying, **both verbally and non-verbally.** Allow them to finish their own sentences and complete their own thoughts.

Do not interrupt. Rest assured that your silence might make them uncomfortable, and they may ask why you are not responding. If that happens, then simply say this: "I didn't want to interrupt you before you finished your thought." While this response shows that you were listening, it also illustrates nonverbally, how you expect to be treated during conversation.

Since you are taking the time to read this book, performing the exercises, and getting in touch with your true and *Purrfectly Authentic*™ self, does it not make sense that you want to date someone that has also taken some time to think about the dating ritual, know who they are, and what they want? Dating someone that has not taken time to discover themselves, whether by utilizing *The 5 Phases* or just having personal introspection, will result in a big bowl of problems later.

Do I really think that people will be willing to answer all these questions about dating, if they believe there are five phases? Probably not, especially if you are expecting them to talk to you in the same manner as one of your friends would. Everyone relates and communicates differently, and no two people are the same. Take time to date the person, and learn their communication style before you get all booed up with them. This will save you plenty of heartache and frustration in the long run.

Anita M. Charlot

Too Much Information (Tmi)

Let's face it, in the beginning many of us tend to talk too much. Some of that is just nervousness, but some of it is because we want the person to get to know us as soon as possible. We want to feed them as much information as possible that will show them how great we are. We want to "keep it 100." We tell them everything that we are looking for in a relationship, including what went wrong in our past relationships, our favorite colors, and even the nature of our relationship with our parents during childhood. We tend to try to find things in common. Because of that, usually the first things we share are the injustices that we have suffered and our wounds.

During the early stages of dating, consider this to be, **too much information.** This person does not need to know these things so soon in the relationship. It's way too much information for a new companion to process. There is a difference between "keeping it 100" and sharing information at the appropriate time. I've heard it put in so many ways:
If they're going to date me, they needs to know exactly who I am.
I want to put it all on the table so that they know what their getting.
- If I tell them how I've been hurt before in the past, they will then know what not to do to keep me happy.
- If they can't handle a strong woman, then they don't need to be with me anyway.
- What you don't realize is that you are playing yourself.

The 5 Phases Of Dating

You're giving them all the information they need to be that "representative" that you are looking for long enough until they feel they have you, and then they will begin to let the real person show. By "keeping it 100" and "spitting the truth," you are coming across in the following way:

- I've been hurt and disappointed before, so I want to tell you everything you need to know so that you won't hurt, disappoint, or leave me too.
- I don't feel confident enough within myself to allow you the opportunity to get to know me.
- I'm tired of the dating scene and I'm ready to settle down ... now!
- Since I told you all the good and bad things about me up front, you don't get to mention them or bring them up again without me saying, 'I told you in the beginning. It shouldn't be anything new.'

Do you see what a difference this is? You may be "keeping it 100" to appear strong, but you're really letting your insecurity and fears show. Dating is about getting to know a person for who they are and allowing them to get to know you, naturally. It should never be forced, and you should never just dump a load of your past on to anyone and expect them to stick around to find out if you were right or not. You always want to have an element of mystery. Give them something to wonder about, to be intrigued about.

Pay attention to the verbal and nonverbal communication methods instead of trying to control the situation. You will begin to notice just how people tend to talk too much in the beginning, volunteering all sorts of information, as well as making promises they can't keep. They stay on the phone for hours once they've move beyond the initial introductory conversation, and instead of ending the conversation there and picking it up later, they continue to talk. At this point, they usually end up saying things that they will not want to be held accountable for later.

In the beginning, you should allow an air of mystery to unfold around you. You want a person to be interested in seeing you again and getting to know more about you. If you give them everything in the beginning, then you will soon run out of things to talk about. There will be no secrets. All your dirty laundry will be aired, and the mystery, along with the mystique, will be gone. Try to sit back and effectively listen. Listen with the intent to hear not only what the person is saying, but also to try to hear what they are not saying.

You can learn a lot about a person by their conversation. You can tell what type of person they are by what they talk about or even how much they talk. What is the nature of their conversation? Do they always seem to be the person that was the saint in each relationship? As they continue to dominate your discussions, do they really have anything of value to say, or are they just filling the silence? Was it always the other person that failed to understand them? Are they always the one to bend more, give more, do more, be more, have more, want more? Pay attention. His or her true nature is showing.

Are they always telling you all about their exes? Do they tell you how much they did for their partner? Do they talk about how much they want to be in a relationship? These are all clues to his or her personality. Verbally they are saying, "It's never my fault." Nonverbally, however, the message is clear that they have not accepted responsibility for their actions, and when things do not go as planned, it is someone else's fault. Having taken the time to get in touch with yourself during the introductory chapters of *The 5 Phases*, you already know what your likes and dislikes are. You have determined the type of person that you feel would be worthy of your emotional energy. Is a person that refuses to accept responsibility on your list? Are you willing to be the reason things don't work out in this relationship, or do you want a partner who can accept responsibility and look at his role in his own failed relationships?

The Importance of Integrity

My definition of a person of integrity is one that knows who they are and communicates that to others. They are honest and sincere and take the time to become familiar with the truth of who they are on a regular basis. Not only do they follow the beat of their own drum, but they also allow and expect others to do likewise. A person of integrity does not ridicule others to make themselves feel better or appear to be superior. They live by the highest code of ethics and have the courage to walk away from anyone or any relationship that does not reflect the same level of integrity.

Why is this important? Because if a person cannot keep their word, finds humor in putting others down, does not respect you or your time, or makes dates and breaks them without consideration of your feelings, then clearly this is not a person of integrity. And if they do not behave with integrity in the very beginning when the dating situation is most vulnerable, what would motivate them to change once there is a commitment?

Talking about the problems in past relationships without giving a clue as to any personal growth that they experienced as a result should be a major red flag. Failure to discuss ways that the problems of their past have helped them to become a better person is usually an indicator that they have not done their homework. For example, I talked about my previous relationships occasionally during my past dating rituals. However, I made sure to point out what I gained from that situation. I am grateful to all my exes because they provided opportunities for growth. Some of the lessons were difficult, but since I was willing to look at myself and do my homework, the person I am today is the culmination of the lessons learned from these experiences.

The most painful relationships provided me with an education that money didn't buy. I appreciate my exes for all our experiences together, for the pain, the infidelity, even the abuse. These experiences led me on the journey to learn more about interpersonal relationships, but most importantly, they taught me to be true to myself-operating only on what was important to my spirit not what other people wanted me to do. I remember sitting across the table from one of my exes, sharing what I wanted to do with my life, how I wanted to own my own business helping other women like myself and how I wanted to write tons of books and facilitate workshops. With her support, I was able to make certain connections within the LGBT community and was encouraged to step outside of my comfort zone. Because of the healing process that I embarked upon after this relationship failed, I found courage again, this time to create the very philosophy that you are reading about today. It was my way of transmuting the energy of my pain into a passion that has lasted over twenty years.

Keep Both Eyes Open

We often get caught up in the "high," the possibility of a new love, or a new relationship, and we think *finally, I have someone to take to family functions that are not just pretending to be my date*; however, we begin to suffer from tunnel vision. Honey, let me inform you: keep both of your eyes open! Pay attention not only to what a person says, but also to what a person does. I know it's an old cliché, but **actions speak louder than words!** Anyone who tells you that they learned from their past, that they have worked through all their issues and now understand themselves better when their actions *clearly* show something different, will give themselves away sooner than later. You must be willing to keep both eyes open to observe and react to what you recognize to be the truth.

If they say one thing, but their actions and their energy tell you something else, you will see their contradictions. And if you happen to call them on this, you will notice that their initial reaction will usually be that of anger, frustration, and then denial. They will cite every book, audio tape, lecture, seminar, or workshop that they have attended, which they hope will prove to you nothing other than they have spent a ton of money running from their real issues. They have built their entire façade around this image that they have created for themselves and will argue to protect their position. Only after beating them over the head with several examples of when they were contradictory will they admit it, *if* you're lucky.

By the time you go through all that drama, having to debate and argue with them to see what they claim does not exist in their world anymore, why would you even consider continuing beyond Phase I with them??? If they are going to battle you over things that are obvious now, what will they do later?

Oh, I'm sorry.

If you like drama, and you feel that unless you are engaging in regular arguments the person doesn't really care about you, then by all means, continue. Fortunately, if you happen to be one of those people, you will still benefit from reading the remainder of this book. You might not be ready at this moment to face your *truth*, but you will undoubtedly learn something along the way.

Understanding a Person's Energy/Spirit

It takes time to really understand a person's true spirit or true personality. In the beginning, everyone is on his or her best behavior. Those of us that have taken the time to get in touch with ourselves are at peace with being where we are and who we are. We know that we are worthy of a wonderful relationship and we do not pretend to be anyone or anything other than who we are. And if we are truly in love with ourselves, what you see is what you get. Now do not get me wrong, even if I am in love with myself and I know who I am, I *still* will not give a new prospect everything in the beginning!

You should be aware that what you see is not always what you get. There is the initial dating persona (the representative) and then there is the real person. In order to really get to know the spirit of another person, you have to spend time with them. You need to see them in different environemts, pay attention to how to talk about other people, listen to how they talk about themselves and their past relationships. Were they always the victim? Were all their ex's crazy? Were they all disrespectful? Comments like these will allow you an inside view to their spirit. It will allow you to "feel their energy."

Does their energy/spirit compliment yours? Does it rub you the wrong way? Do their actions, responses or behaviors go against your morals? Paying attention to these things up front will save you a lot of headache and possible arguments later. Rush through this process and you can guarantee it will become more problematic later.

Respect of Time and Space

When we meet someone and there is a mutual interest, we want to spend as much time as possible with them, learning about them, trying to figure out if we want to "apply for the job," or making sure we are even a good candidate for an interview. This type of behavior borders on desperation. In Phase I, you are still just trying to figure out if this person has enough of the positive things on your lists for you to want to move to Phase II. Do not jump the gun.

Keep your regular schedule. Do not make yourself readily available all the time for this person. Do not lose sight of the things that you want to do just yet; this is not the stage where you would start rearranging your schedule. First, you need to determine if the person is even worth it.

The Bus Stops Here

If after several conversations with this person you recognize that they would not be potential dating material, but possibly a friend to socialize with occasionally, then just be honest with them. Pull the signal cord on the bus and get off at the next stop. Do not waste *your* time and be considerate enough not to waste the other person's time. Each case will be different, as some people will tell you that they are okay with being just friends, while at the same time, behaving as though they are still interested in more. You must make that call; however, the more in touch with yourself you are, the more capable you are to understand the other person's intentions.

PHASE II: DATING, BUT NOT EXCLUSIVELY - SURVEYING THE LANDSCAPE

Proposed Timeline: 3-6 Months

This will be the longest period of the first three phases. Here is where you begin to roll up your sleeves and get your hands dirty. In this phase, you are surveying the landscape. You are dating with the intention and mindset of learning more about the potential candidates to determine which one will be the person you choose with whom to invest your time, energy, and your heart. This is also the phase where we tend to smudge the lines a bit. Here is where we tend to get a little cloudy and a little fuzzy on what our expectations are and what the expectations of the other person should be. Please pay attention here, as this is certain to shake up some of the potentials, while validating the others.

All Dating Situations Are Not Potential Relationships!!!

How many times have I repeated this to my friends as well as my clients? I continue to hear the same insecurity issues being brought up in this phase. Questions like these arise:
What if they do not like me as much as I like them?
What if I am not the only person that they are dating?
I am tired of this whole dating thing. Why do I have to continue to play this game?

- Why doesn't he tell me if he is not really looking for a relationship?
- What does it mean if he talked to me on Saturday but

The 5 Phases Of Dating

it's Tuesday and I still haven't heard from him?
- Why?
- What if?
- Would he?
- Why did he do xyz?

All dating situations are not potential relationships. Now say it with me: **ALL DATING SITUATIONS ARE NOT POTENTIAL RELATIONSHIPS!** Why do we act so desperate? Girl, I am speaking directly to you!!! Why is it that women tend to feel they cannot have a dating situation without it developing into a relationship?

Let us take a peek at what the concept of dating is, according to *The 5 Phases*. **Dating** is an opportunity to get to know several different men. **Dating** is a time to understand more about them and yourself as you interact together. **Dating** is where you take the time to tweak your three lists as you learn more about yourself through this ritual. Now if this is what the whole concept of dating is all about, then why is it commonplace to begin developing an attitude of being exclusive, seeing only one person at one time? Why do we insist on trying to make the "relationship" work just because we have been spending our time with someone for the past several months? Lesson: **Do not place yourself in such a tight box with these restrictions and do not allow anyone else to do that to you either.**

Interview Phase

If we were to look at the dating ritual in Phase II (as

accepting job applications), and if you were an employer hiring a new employee for a position, would you only interview one candidate, even though they did not meet the majority of your criteria, then allow them to believe they were the only person you were interviewing? Would it not be better to let them know that you were still accepting applications and that you would call them back for another interview if their experience met the requirements?

Although I am not a huge fan of reality shows, I do think the ones featuring the bachelor or bachelorette who is required to date and get to know twenty eligible prospects, while showing it on national television are actually onto something. My annoyance with these programs is watching how vulnerable some of the women are and seeing how far they are willing to go in their pursuit of catching a man. Sometimes they go so far that it is degrading to witness (from a female perspective, I think). However, the main theme that I appreciate from these shows is that they are open and honest about the need to date several different people until they find the one that is right for them.

During these types of programs, the audience watches clips of how the contestant spent time with each prospect in several different situations, while at the same time cross-referencing their behavior, conversations, and energy with the contestants' internal three lists. After a certain amount of time, they choose the one that best fits whatever they are looking for. Hopefully it is also one that they have developed true and honest feelings for. Now, my personal conflict is this: why is it that some people will glorify a scenario of twenty women or men, who very well realize they are kissing the same person on

The 5 Phases Of Dating

a television show, yet in everyday life act as if it is a crime to date more than one person, when they are **not** yet committed?

The system is ridiculous. It is essential for you to date several different prospects in Phase II, and it is important to let them know that they are not the only person that you are dating. Why? Because it gives a realistic picture of what is going on. There are no hidden agendas and no unrealistic expectations. I am often asked about physical contact during Phase II. If it should take place, then what is considered Phase II contact? How long should you wait? Stay tuned. I will get to this later.

Dating Multiple People?

This is my favorite and most controversial section of Phase II. Should you date more than one person at a time? **Absolutely!** Should you let the individuals know that you are dating several people? **Absolutely!** Should you answer any questions about your dating situations? **Use your judgement.** If someone asks questions like, *what phases are you in with other prospects?* or *Where do they fall in the pecking order?* Well, I think you should be as honest as you are prepared to be. I have found that going through my initial dating stage before choosing my next relationship made dating more refreshing and stress free. Have you seen Spike Lee's remake of *She's Gotta Have It*? When I saw the original years ago, I was in a different head space; however, this time around I fell in love with Nola's character. Not because she was so darned cute, but because she was a dramatization of exactly what this section is about: **dating more than one person at a time, while being honest with**

each of them.

You can be in several different phases at a time with as many people as you can juggle. Whether you are physical with all of them is a personal choice that you have to make. The key is to be honest about the fact that you are dating different people until you find that one true individual that provides enough of the qualities you feel are conducive to establishing a long-term relationship. And if you **do** decide to be physical with more than one of them, be safe about it.

Be aware that not everyone will be able to handle this information; not everyone is okay with competition. Knowing that they are not #1 on your dating prospects list can bring out a person's hidden insecurities. However, not having to worry about covering your tracks, lying about what you are doing, or making up stories about why you weren't available when they called, allows you the freedom that is necessary to make the decision that is best for you. For example, when I was on the market I was usually dating 2-3 people at any given time. This may seem like a lot to some of you; however, let me add that I was not physically attracted or physically involved with more than one at a time. Dating does not mean engaging in sexual activity, and I hope that not all your dating situations have this element. I was very careful about whom, how, when, and at what time I allowed myself to go there with someone. From a metaphysical perspective, each person you are intimate with leaves an imprint of their spirit with you and takes a little imprint of yours with them. As you saw in *She's Gotta Have It*, Nola's spirit was depleted. She had given so much of herself away to the men in her life, which allowed them to plug into her "power source." The consequence? She barely knew who **she** was. Don't

The 5 Phases Of Dating

let this be you.

People I dated at that time were fully aware they weren't the only ones. I was clear with them at what phase of the dating process I felt we were in. As we moved from one phase to another, we communicated and agreed that we were both in fact on the same page. Therefore, we had no misunderstandings. I laugh each time I remember this statement made by one of my Phase II individuals. The straight to the point question was, "I understand that we are not exclusively dating; however, I need to know if we are exclusively *&^%'ing?" I could only laugh. It was a valid question that deserved an honest answer. I reassured her that it was an exclusive physical relationship.

My roommate at the time observed me living *The 5 Phases of Dating* philosophy. We spent endless nights talking about. She would say, "I'm not good at project managing." I never thought I was either; however, it is a necessary skill set to date several different people at one time. The easiest way to do this is to be honest. Do not give away too much information about other potentials. When asked the question of whether I was sexually active with the other potentials, my answer was short and quick, "When, and if, we get to that point in our dating situation where that becomes a valid question, I will answer it then." This may seem evasive to some, but unless you are considering becoming sexually active with the person that asked the question, what you do with others is between you and them.

Anita M. Charlot

Keep Shopping

Dating several people at the same time is equivalent to going to the mall looking for that perfect outfit. In order to have the outfit of your dreams, several pieces are necessary, and you may have to go to several stores to find them all. For example, if you already know exactly what item you are looking for, it will shorten the amount of time you need to spend shopping. You know exactly what style you are looking for; however, you will know the actual pieces when you see them.

Let us say you decide to shop at Mall A. After spending some time there, you may find a nice top and a pair of earrings to match, but your outfit is still incomplete. What you have discovered is that Mall A is good for tops and jewelry, but it does not necessarily have everything that you want. While going on with your life and enjoying Mall A for what it has to offer, you happen to hear about Mall B through a friend. You decide to check out Mall B only to discover that this mall not only has great slacks and shoes, but to your surprise it also has a good selection of jewelry. Do you stop shopping at Mall A? No! Mall A is still a possibility when you are in the mood for what it has to offer. Once at Mall B, do you let them know that you are still shopping around? Of course, you do. Who does not like a healthy dose of competition? Men do not appreciate or value women who come too easy. This doesn't mean that you have to play games, but, the more you value yourself, the more they will value you. Don't be a fool for love. Doing so will put you in a position to be played with.

Stay with me now. Remember, you still do not have a complete outfit. What would be ideal is to find something close

The 5 Phases Of Dating

to, or even better than what you set out looking for in the first place. You are looking for a complete outfit, one that will dress you from head to toe, yet you still must find a mall that can satisfy all of your needs, wants, and desires. So, what is a girl to do? Keep shopping! When you are in the mood for jewelry and tops, go to Mall A. When you are in the mood for slacks, shoes, and a little jewelry, go to Mall B. Wait, you have just run across Mall C, which happens to have a wide selection of skirts, and hair and nail salons, but it does not have the tops, slacks, or shoes that you are looking for. Do you not shop there because you are already "involved" with two other malls? No, you shop there when you are in the mood for what it can provide.

My point is simple. Given the mall example, just as you have taken the time to get in touch with what you want in a perfect outfit for the evening, then you **should** also take the time to decide what you want in the perfectly imperfect mate. The analogy may be a little implausible, but the concept remains the same. You would not stop going to a mall because you could not find everything that you wanted there, so why would you dump the first person you decide to date because they do not have everything you're looking for? When the second person comes along that just happens to have a little more to offer that does not mean you have to dump the first one, and so on.

The whole idea of dating is so that you have different types of experiences with different personalities until you find the one that best resonates with the quality and caliber of that perfectly imperfect person you want in your life. You will not find this person by avoiding the dating scene all together, by being dishonest with yourself, by not clearly understanding what it is you really want in a mate, or by settling for the first person that decides to pay you some attention. No one likes to be around a clingy and desperate individual. Placing all your eggs in one basket or only shopping at Mall A when clearly not all required items are present is a mistake on your part, which robs you of valuable lessons that you will learn along the way. Indulge yourself. There are thirty-one plus flavors of Baskin Robbins ice cream, so why would you only settle for vanilla?

Me Time

I cannot stress enough how important it is not to lose sight of yourself. Continue to have your time, time to refer to this book, the day in the life of your Perfect Relationship Story, and your three lists. Also make time for meditation and physical exercise. Do whatever it takes to stay grounded and in touch with yourself. Dating can be fun and adventurous, but it can also be a distraction, keeping you from your most important relationship: the one you have with yourself. **You should always come first.** Take time to go inside and think about your conversations with this person and about your feelings when you talk with him or her.

Do they contradict themselves often? Do you notice any differences in what they say and what they do? Do you notice that you are giving your power away to this person? Are you acting desperate? You should contemplate these things on a regular basis; no one is more important than you are. Do not make the mistake of putting the other person first in the beginning. Trust me. It will never be your turn later. Your turn will rarely come, if at all. As my mother used to say, "Don't start nothing you don't plan on finishing."

The 5 Phases Of Dating

Creating the Blueprint

Phase II is when the blueprint for the foundation of a relationship is created. How is this person measuring up according to your three lists and your Perfect Relationship Story? Do you see things in this person that attract you but were not considered when you made your lists? Does this person surprise you with more positive qualities than he or she disappoints you with negative ones? Pay attention and keep a mental note. You are not necessarily keeping track, but staying fully awake. You want to be aware of what you are working with here. Keep these thoughts in the back of your mind:

- How do they treat other people that they do not know?
- What is their relationship like with their family?
- How are they around their friends?
- Are they constantly gossiping judging or condemning other people?
- Is their conversation shallow and meaningless to you?
- Are you able to talk about the things that are most important to you?
- Do you have similar interests?
- What are your spiritual beliefs, if any? Will they clash?
- Are they open to learning new things?
- Are they willing at least to peek into your world, to learn what makes you tick, what makes you happy, or how you came to be the person that you are today?

These are all very important factors when considering a long-term relationship with someone. If you do not feel as though the person is genuinely interested in who you are now, and you don't have common interests or goals at this stage, what is the point of making a formal commitment to each other? You are free to stay in Phase II as long as necessary, but then again if it is a relationship that you are looking for, and the one you are in is not working, then it is important that you move on and find a person that will be more compatible with your needs and desires.

Deceptive Advertising

Here we go again. You have just recently met the person who you consider the person of your dreams, right? The two of you hit it off immediately as they have so many of the qualities you wanted in a partner. The chemistry is there. They are thoughtful and considerate. The flowers, cards, and trinkets have continued for several months now, and you have a strong case of the "warm-n-fuzzies." To top it all off, the sex is the bomb!!!

So, what have you done? The very thing we all tend to do. You have begun to let your guard down. You've opened up about things that you would not have otherwise shared. You have hinted around to the fact that they can call you anytime. You've cleared your calendar and made yourself available whenever they called. You have even cancelled plans with your friends and family at the last minute to be with them. And then out of nowhere...BAM! Things have started to change.

You've noticed that they seem to be a little more moody than usual. You've noticed that they did not return your calls, texts, IMs, DMs, or hangouts as quickly as they used to.

The 5 Phases Of Dating

Suddenly, they have become too tired to get together. They've started using family members as excuses for not being able to see you, or suddenly, they need to be there for their friends. Believe me, they can instantly become "Martha Stewart creative" with their excuses.

Things were going great at first, then all of a sudden, they started to change. What did you do? Did you say the wrong thing? Did you ask too many questions? Did you put too much pressure on them? The answer to these questions is very simple. You did **absolutely nothing**! It is human nature during the dating game to put forth so much effort and energy in the beginning. Everything is new. We are on our best behavior. The first three months are blissful because it's the honeymoon phase of a new, potential relationship. We behave as though we are on a new job and need to make it past our 90-day probationary period.

It is my experience that the first three months are the greatest. During the second three months, a person tends to feel like the initial dating phase is over and they can now start to relax. Things go unnoticed. The time they want to spend with you is leveling out, and they start to work other activities and people back into their schedules. They feel confident of being a "shoe-in" for the job; therefore, they begin to slack off. In the second three months, the **real** person starts to shine through. The person that is now truly confident that they have invested enough time and energy into the relationship appears, and they don't have to worry about doing the very things that attracted you to them in the first place.

This, my friend, is what I call Deceptive Advertising. Stop what you are doing right now and rush to the phone to call the B.B.B. (Biggest Bull-Shitter Bureau). What you see is not always what you get. People like to make themselves out to be the brightest and the best thing walking the earth. They want all the positives and potential information that others might be looking for to help them stand apart from the crowd. So, they bend the truth a little bit, make things seem a lot more important than they really are, and claim to be a particular way when, in fact, they are not. They may drive a new car, own several pieces of real estate, and talk about travels to exotic places to present themselves as a particular package. If you wait it out long enough, the truth will eventually come out.

Most of us have been guilty of this at some point in our lives. We want to be the **chosen one**; we want to place ourselves above the rest of the would-be's, so we tend to twist the truth a bit. Is this right? No, it is not! However, it is a part of the dating game. So, you may be wondering what we can do about it? Well, for starters, you can continue to get to know a person for at least three months without becoming too emotionally or physically wrapped up in them. Know that everyone will slow down on the dating rituals between the third and fourth months, but wait and see what emerges after that.

Even with the best intentions, it is common to play this game in one fashion or another. The trick is to be aware that it is a pattern in the ritual of dating and to be patient enough to see how comfortable you feel with this person after the honeymoon period ends. Remember, you can end a dating situation whenever you feel it is necessary, so never feel obligated or stuck in a situation. Even if you have invested time, money, and energy, whether the dating situation led to an actual relationship or not, you learned more about yourself, your likes, dislikes, and what you are and are not willing to compromise on for the sake of a relationship. If for no other reason, this has made time with the other person valuable.

Do not believe everything you hear! I cannot stress this enough. I have fallen into this trap far too many times not to mention it here. In the dating arena, as much as we would like to think that people are always honest and forthcoming, that is not always the case. When you are trying to get someone to like you, or you have determined that a person is someone that you can see building a relationship with, you tend to say all the right things, make all of the right moves, and operate like a well-oiled machine. You put on your "job face" because you are determined to be hired for this position. Pay attention and stay alert!

The Reality of Finances

While writing the first version of this book, I found myself unemployed and having to reevaluate my life due to monumental changes. In an effort to learn more about myself and the differences between my partners and me, I discovered great insight in relation to money. It was a true epiphany for me, one that shed a necessary light on my constant state of affairs and why I repeated certain patterns. Having said that, let's take a few minutes to review *your* relationship to money.

Do you have enough to take care of your basic survival needs? Do you have a little extra cash to treat yourself on occasion? Do you have a modest nest egg set aside for a rainy day? Or do you have a huge retirement fund and personal savings account that you can take pride in?

What is your relationship to this money? Are you a spendthrift or a shop-a-holic (did someone say shoe sale?) What are your financial goals, dreams, and aspirations? What does your financial future look like? What is your credit score (FICO score)? What animal comes to mind when you think of your credit report: a proud lion or a helpless field mouse? Why in the world should this topic come up in this book you may ask? That's easy to answer since many relationships, including marriages, end due to arguments and differences in opinion about money.

While money is important to me, I'm not obsessed with it. Don't get me wrong, I know that money is truly important, and everyone needs to have it and enough of it, but I don't allow it to be the nucleus of everything that I do, have, or want to be. I always tell people that I am more concerned about what is going on inside a person. I watch the internal market, making sure that I have invested enough time and energy into the proper areas for me: mental, emotional, and spiritual. As I watch those stocks grow in a positive direction, the result will manifest on the outside, including in the financial arena.

> *For what shall it profit a man, if he shall gain the whole world, and lose his own soul?*
> (Mark 8:36, King James Version)

So, let's take a moment to answer some reality questions regarding your future. Where are you financially? Where is your partner (or potential partner)? What are **your** future dreams that relate to your financial or credit standing? What financial personality type is your partner? Are you comfortable with where they are? Will you expect certain things out of them later or during the relationship that you're afraid to talk about now? Is this the time to talk about it? What about where you are financially? If what you want is a partner that is financially secure and has good credit, then are you bringing the same thing to the table? Are you looking for a partner that can take care of themselves only? How about one that can take care of themselves but also has the means and the willingness to take care of you too if something happened that caused you to become "financially strapped" temporarily? These questions are important. At this point, I'm not saying that you share copies of your credit report or bank statements with one another. This isn't the time for that.

What I am saying is that you need to get a good, clear, and honest understanding of where you are and what you want prior to committing to a relationship with someone. Also, if you are okay with where they are at that moment, then make sure that you will be okay with them being there in the future. In a perfect world, they would learn from you or you would both agree to let the person that was stronger in the financial area handle the finances. However, there is nothing better than clear insight and open communication that will save you and your relationship from a lot of trouble. If necessary and for your own sake, get your finances in order, not just for your relationship, but also for yourself. You will feel better about you if you do.

Anita M. Charlot

Money Talks

This is a very touchy subject to me as I'm sure it is to a lot of you. Personally, I don't like talking about my finances with anyone. I feel so exposed, so vulnerable. I am currently working on changing my relationship to money. That means my relationship with sharing my financial place in life as well.

I have not been a person of great financial wealth. Lord knows I have had many financial challenges and emotional issues related to money. Therefore, I have not been quick to share this information with anyone. Initially, my desire was to have someone in my life that was in a better place than I was financially, someone who could hold their own and support my dreams, if necessary. What I have since learned is that I'm not comfortable with the idea of someone taking care of me as it puts me in a position of feeling as though I must kiss ass to maintain the relationship. And ass-kissing isn't something that I'm good at. Let's just say that it's at the top of my *Hell Naw* list.

If what you want is someone that is financially sound with perfect credit, then you need to be that as well. If you are not currently in that position, then work on getting there. There is nothing like the energy of money clouding an otherwise healthy relationship. Discover your relationship to money and you will free yourself from that "cloud of doom." Also, if you have not done so already, get copies of your credit report from the three bureaus (TransUnion, Equifax, and Experian) to begin to clear things up that negatively impact your score and to pay others off, if possible. There are also several great books available to help

The 5 Phases Of Dating

you organize, prepare, and repair your credit and financial standing for all types of relationships, both straight and alternative.

If you're not financially independent, then you might end up with Big D*ck Willie. You know the type. They front with what they have: money, cars, condos, homes, vacations, all to impress you. They spend money lavishly on you in the beginning, while secretly holding a grudge against you because you accept it. Beware of the man that wants to lead with his wallet. Some men will give you their wallet, their credit cards, their bodies, their car keys, before (if ever) giving you his heart. Don't get caught up in the sparkle of a man spending so much money on you to the point where you lower your standards, or you begin to put up with disrespectful behavior because he feels he owns you. This is a slippery slope indeed, and each situation is different. Just be careful. The misplaced anger at you for accepting the gifts is a sign of him trying to overcompensate for something that he has yet to deal with. Let him practice on someone else.

Let's Talk Honesty

The main reason we fall short of finding that *Purrfectly Authentic*™ relationship is a simple four-letter word: **FEAR**.
- Fear of rejection;
- Fear of humiliation;
- Fear of not getting what we want;

- Fear of being hurt again;
- Fear of sounding stupid;
- Fear of being vulnerable;
- Fear of the unknown;
- Fear of losing a potential prospect; and
- Fear of a whole host of "hypothetical situations."

Fear will cause you to lose the very thing that you say you want. Fear will cause you to accept the first person that comes along instead of waiting for that person that resonates more with your spirit. Fear will cause you to sabotage yourself. Why are we so fearful of being honest with others and ourselves? I'll tell you why: **change!**

    Being honest with yourself and with others increases the possibility that things will change: the nature of friendships, relationships, both familial and intimate, your work environment, and your affiliations with organizations. Once you get in touch with your truth, you will begin to see the things you put up with for all the wrong reasons. Once you are aware of what you currently have in your life versus what you truly desire, you can neither hide behind those dark shades of unawareness that have been holding you back, nor can you continue to play the victim. When you become aware, you will no longer continue to deprive yourself of the things that free your spirit and your mind.

    Again, fear is the problem that needs to be cured: fear of the unknown. And as you begin developing this newly discovered information database, some questions may begin to arise, such as:

- Now that I have identified my **truth**, what do I do

The 5 Phases Of Dating

with this new information?
- How will the people that are close to me receive this new information?
- Will this change my relationships?
- If I articulate my true needs and desires, will they still want to be with?
- Will the person leave me?
- Will I be rejected, ridiculed, or attacked?

We usually meet the idea of change with trepidation. Up until now, you have allowed society, your family, and your previous relationships and friendships to determine who you are. You've allowed fear to push those close to you away, to determine how you behaved, what you accepted and what you tolerated. You've acted big and bad by being the person to walk away first, so that you wouldn't have to deal with the pain. We have all put up with situations, behaviors, and people that we knew were toxic for us, because we felt that it was the right thing to do.

Now, **what are you going to do**? You have taken the time to go on a journey inside of yourself and find out what your spirit truly desires. You are now aware of what is missing. What do you do with this information?

The façade that you have been hiding behind all this time should become obvious to you. You have two choices now:
1. Remain stuck with your current lifestyle and continually miss the opportunity to live a more realistic life based on your newly found **truth**, or
2. Set out to live your life according to what you have recognized and discovered as your true nature and

learn how to relate from that.

Either way you will never be the same. You may begin to recognize that your friendship with a particular person has been one-sided all this time. It might become apparent that you've been taken advantage of. You may realize that you merely **exist** in several of your relationships, or that your relationship no longer feeds your spirit.

Being in touch with your **true** self gives you an inner confidence that you might not have had otherwise. Knowing who you are, what you want, what you don't want, and recognizing that you're worthy, puts you in control of your relationship destiny. You are no longer just going through the motions, allowing yourself to be taken on an emotional rollercoaster based on the mood swings of others, or operating out of fear and desperation. You are now empowered to choose the relationship that you want instead of crossing your fingers waiting to be the one chosen.

From this place of confidence, your fears are no longer in control. You are no longer blindly led by your apprehension that you cannot have what you want. In contrast, you begin to believe that it's possible to have anything your heart and spirit desire. From this place you are better able to articulate your needs, wants, and desires with confidence, knowing if it doesn't manifest itself in the person that you're currently dating, then that special someone is somewhere within our realm. **PLEASE NOTE**: Do not fall into the desperate notion of *something is better than no*thing. I would much rather spend quality time alone, enjoying my own company than being in the company of someone that makes me feel inferior or has me second-guessing them and myself all too often.

The 5 Phases Of Dating

Doing Your Research

This area should be taken very seriously. Learning as much as you can about someone in the beginning will give you a better chance of making the right decision in the end. You want to see how this person behaves in as many scenarios as possible: when they have a pocket full of money, when they are down to their last dime, when they are in a good/sad/angry mood, and when they interact with their family, friends, and even the server at the restaurant. Pay attention to how they react when they are under pressure, how they handle their quiet time. All these things are very important in choosing your life partner. If he has children, then what is the relationship like with him and his child's mother? Does he have a relationship with his child? If not, what is the story behind it? If you have children or want to have children someday, then what is his view of parenting? What does he believe a parent's role is? What will he think **his** role will be in your child's life?

I have often made the mistake of not following my own 3-6-9 rule and getting into committed relationships before I have taken the time to see the person for who they really were. How can you avoid this often overlooked step? **By taking your time to date the person!** That's how. There is no need to rush anything. Know that in the beginning, the person that you see is not all there is. There is a lot more! After spending time with that individual, you will be able to determine whether your spirits will be good for one another.

Anita M. Charlot

Cat/Dog Theory

In *The Mastery of Love* (Ruiz 1999), one particular section hit me right between the eyes: his cat/dog theory. He uses the analogy of a cat and a dog to explain an aspect of the dating ritual. Even though we want a cat, we will settle for a dog, and then complain that he won't meow. On the other hand, when we want to date a dog (no pun intended), we will date a cat and then get angry because the cat will not bark.

How many times have you dated someone that did not treat you a particular way in the beginning, only to complain about them not doing that particular thing for you later on in the relationship? Admit it. Most of us are guilty of doing this.

I remember a situation when dating several people concurrently, who I thought would learn from the way that I treated them, and by some magical love spell would then treat me the same way in return. **Not!** If it walks like a dog, barks likes a dog, scratches fleas like a dog, then damn it, it's a dog!!! Do not continue to date the dog and complain that he just will not meow for you. They will not rub up against you softly, or purr in your ear. If they were loud and boisterous in the beginning, then they will be loud and boisterous for every other time in the middle. If they were rude and/or made rude comments to you in the beginning, even after you asked them not to, then **trust,** they will continue to make those rude comments to you in the future. I am not stating that you cannot find some happiness with this person; however, you should take time to really get to know who/what you are dating in the beginning. Then when you see the person for the character that they truly are, you will not be so caught up or surprised that you cannot walk away from the situation. There is no law that states because you spent time with this person (weeks, months, or even years), that you are required to stick with them.

Being in Phase II is all about shopping around as my mother used to tell me. Remember, you are surveying the landscape. If you found that a piece of land that you wanted to purchase to build your home was unstable, full of damaging material, or your SEROI (Spiritual and Emotional Rate of Investment) was entirely too high, then you would not purchase it and build your house anyway, would you? Then, why continue to remain in a dating situation where your SEROI was not proportionate to your SEROR (Spiritual and Emotional Rate of Return)? Move on to the next piece of property.

Leave the Drama at the Door

Do the following statements sound familiar? *I know we don't spend enough time together, but they are always busy. He has baby-mama issues. Their ex cheated on them. Their parents were abusive. Their ex just can't seem to let go of the relationship. They have to have contact with the ex, or he or she will harm themselves.* **Stop the Madness**! There are too many issues on the table before you can even get started. If you find yourself in a similar situation to the above soap operas, then let this individual get themselves together first. **PLEASE**. The last thing you need is a bunch of drama before you even get off the ground and running.

Anita M. Charlot

If The Train Doesn't Stop At Your Station, Then It's Not Your Train!!!

I had the pleasure of meeting Marianne Williamson, one of my favorite authors, in person. She is such a wonderful woman with an honest spirit. She is also known for this famous phrase, "If the train doesn't stop at your station, it's not your train!" Marianne Williamson is known throughout the metaphysical community for her down to earth way of breaking down the bible and *A Course in Miracles* and showing us how it applies to our everyday lives, including relationships. This statement alone screams loud and clear. *If the train does not stop at your station, then it's not your train* speaks volumes to those who sit back and sulk about not being the chosen one picked for their partner.

Her point is very simple. If the person that you are interested in is not interested in you, then they're not the person for you. Quit sitting in the train station waiting for that train to stop and pick you up. Continue to live and grow, and trust that a train will eventually stop in your station. And when it does, it will be the right train, the right time, and you'll have the correct fare. Let go of past relationships and crushes, and get on with your life. As long as you hold on to that old possibility, you're blocking the track for the train that is meant for you to pull in.

The 5 Phases Of Dating

Let It Go!

Okay, let us say you have been practicing the phases and you recognize that a person that you've been dating is no longer someone that you want to progress any further. What do you do? How do you handle this? Quite simply, with **honesty**! I remember some dating situations in the past where I was afraid of telling the person that it was not going to work. I did not want to hurt their feelings. I figured if I just ignored their phone calls, always stayed busy, broke dates, and stood them up, then they would eventually get the hint. Why I thought these behaviors would not hurt their feelings is beyond me. Then, I had the nerve to get upset when people were not upfront with me and treated me the same way that I had done others. Most people do not like rejection or confrontation. The personality type of the person that you are dealing with plays a part as well in how you choose to handle the situation. I was in Phase II with two separate individuals, and after having spent an adequate amount of time with both, I determined that neither one of them possessed what was needed to sustain a long-term relationship with me. Here are three different examples:

Example #1

After careful analysis, I realized that she and I were on opposite ends of the spectrum. I tried to explain the difference between our personalities. I was as tactful and nonjudgmental as I could possibly be. She was not angry, but she interpreted what I'd said as if I meant something was wrong with her.

I continued to reiterate our differences: I operated more from my spirit; she operated from her personality. I was not concerned with what other people thought of my actions or me; she lived by other peoples' opinions of her. I was not confrontational and enjoyed constructive criticism; she wanted to debate everything and was in complete denial. This shopping experience did not warrant further investigation. It was clear that I would not be happy with her.

I was continuously met with phrases like, "I'll change. I can fix that. Don't put me back to Phase I. I understand now. I'm sorry. Give me another chance." What she did not understand was that there was no possible way that she could have changed enough to be in alignment with my spirit or with what I really needed. Any attempt on her part to do so would only have taken her even further from living her own **truth**, and eventually she would be tired of playing the game, and then resent me for having "changed her" while fighting every minute of it.

It was clear that her feelings were hurt and she felt rejected. She continued to ask me questions as to why she would not be the one I chose, and I was very honest with her. It did not feel good to either of us. A couple of months went by, and I received a wonderful email from her telling me how much she appreciated my honesty, and that as a result, she sat down, reviewed our conversation and the things I pointed out. In the end, both of us had learned a lot about ourselves in the process.

She stated that no one had ever pointed those things out to her before, and while they were hard to hear, and she fought me tooth and nail about their validity, she later realized that they were true. As she ended the letter, she told me that being

The 5 Phases Of Dating

completely honest with her was the best gift she could have received from me because it allowed her to get in touch with her **own truth**. This was not easy for her or for me, but ultimately, it was appreciated. It felt good to know that I had been instrumental in her growth as she had been in mine, while at the same time remaining true to what I really wanted.

Example #2

This was a Phase II dating situation, accompanied by maintenance. Let me define maintenance for you: *Maintenance is a mutually agreed upon sexual arrangement, ideally with no expectations.* Now, this is not an easy concept for everyone. In the end, this individual was not strong enough to handle maintenance. During the dating ritual, I was very clear about the Phases, what was acceptable and unacceptable, and what my intentions were.

Before we began the maintenance portion, I was very clear in explaining that just because there was maintenance involved, that did not mean it would result in a future relationship. We discussed this in detail and both agreed. As time went on, I noticed that there were signs of not being able to handle the maintenance aspect without a relationship part.

If I did not return a call when she wanted, she was shady with me. If I did not allocate more time to spend with her, she was shady with me. Suddenly, there were unspoken expectations, none of them part of the deal. As the difference between what she said she could handle and what she could not became painfully apparent, I decided to have a talk with her.

During this conversation, she stated that she was starting to develop strong feelings for me because of our intimacy. She told me that I was on some "ghetto-bullshit," thinking that we could be intimate without having our feelings involved, and that I was just cold-hearted. I reminded her of what we had agreed to in the beginning and how clear I was about what I wanted and what I did not want, about our initial agreement before commencement. She proceeded to tell me that she could not help it, that it just happened.

At that point, I told her that it was obvious that she could not handle the maintenance portion of the situationship, and as a result, it would have to stop. I see this as an area that more women tend to get caught up in than men do. Women are known for attaching their heart to physical intimacy, while men can remain detached. I just happen to be one of the few women that think like a man in this area. Maintenance is just that in my opinion, maintenance, nothing more! If you called the plumber out to your house to fix the sink, it is an agreement. A service agreement in which once the service is performed, and the deal is done, the plumber leaves. Purpose fulfilled. Do you then get upset when the plumber doesn't text you a few days later? Do you take it personal? Maintenance is the same way. If you are not in the right head/heart space to deal with maintenance, then avoid it.

If you are not one of those women that can keep your feelings separate from your sexual encounters, then it's best not to have them. Needless to say, once I recognized that she could not handle the maintenance agreement, I knew that I had to end things. I could have continued to have my needs taken care of with little respect for her feelings, but that is not me. Once I

The 5 Phases Of Dating

realized that she was unable to continue according to our original understanding I could no longer be intimate with her. I would always know in the back of my mind that she was hoping for more.

We had a good time together. She showered me with gifts and treated me like a queen; however, she was not the **one**, and no amount of maintenance was going to change that. Our interaction/conversation ended for about two months after, and then she called, and we very calmly and intelligently brought closure to our dating situation. We recognized that a good friendship was something with which we could both be comfortable.

Example #3

He was a very intelligent and educated man. He caught me completely off guard. I listened to him talk about his travels, his plans to work abroad in India, his two master's degrees, the three plus occasions when he attended relationship seminars, how his mother was a strong black woman and how much she and I were alike. I just knew this one would be different.

He was different. He had never lived with anyone other than during a vacation. He was in his 40's and had never married. He had no children, and he had just recently walked away from a four-year relationship that was unsatisfactory to him for a long time. So, what attracted me to him? I was looking for a savior, someone to save me from my negative experiences with men in my past. I just knew that he would come along and be a great father/role model for my children, encourage me, and show me the life that I had longed for, the one he had been living.

He was six years older than I was. In a way, he was very interesting because he had been sheltered from the usual drama associated with the men that I had been involved with. He was very polished, yet very humble. He had jobs with salaries I had only dreamed about, and he was smart. He could put on a business suit and look clean as hell, then after hours throw on some Timberland boots and a long sleeve t-shirt and look like a brotha from the neighborhood. He was "perfect," or so I imagined.

I felt as though I could allow myself to be submissive with this type of man. Why you may ask? Because he deserved it! He ran my bathwater after I had had a long day. He would even clean the tub for me. He took me to wonderful new places for dinner. He described what we were going to do together, the trips he would take me on, the things he would show me. He would make me toasted peanut butter and jelly sandwiches before I left for school (okay, put that eyebrow down, I was going to college at night right after work). He always looked out for me. He would occasionally hand me a few dollars for lunch. It was great.

I was so tired of doing everything and having to be responsible for everything, that I was eager to turn some of my responsibilities over to him. He was very respectful. He always treated me like a woman. He was the perfect gentleman. He loved his mother, and he would tell me how I reminded him of her because of her strength to rise above single parenthood and the stigma that came along with it. I felt so understood and respected.

After a while, I noticed the dinners slowed down. I was now running my own bathwater and getting my own

The 5 Phases Of Dating

wine. The initial dating phase/the honeymoon phase was over, and we had crossed the three-month threshold. It was disappointing. I thought he was different. All the while, I continued to be consistent-consistently untrue to my spirit. I figured things would slow down a bit. He is a good brother, so I cut him some slack. But deep down inside, something was not right. I recognized that the grand promises that were made in the beginning were not being kept. I realized that while this brother had attended all these seminars about relationships, the true work of introspection, awareness, and change had not been completed yet. While he had been free with his home, his vehicle, his wallet, and his sex, he was not going to reveal his emotions anytime soon. It was obvious to me that there were some deep-rooted issues surrounding love and pain that he was completely closed off to.

    I started to get angry with him for not being the man he led me to believe he was in the beginning. We argued. I left town for a week. He called apologizing, showing the first sign of emotion. He said he missed me. That was music to my ears, finally, a sign of emotion. Forget the fact that I was out of town and that we had argued before I left: he had opened up!

    He was such a nice guy that I struggled with whether it was me that was asking for/looking for too much, or if it was he that promised the world, yet did not deliver. After arguing with him and not talking to him for a while, I realized that it really was not his fault. I so desperately wanted him to be the one that would erase all the misery and pain I had experienced with the other men in my life that no matter what he did, he would always come short.

Once I recognized this, I apologized to him. I wrote him a long letter and explained why I was angry, why I initially felt justified in my anger, and the epiphany that I had surrounding how I projected my needs onto him. Of course, he was the one to make all the promises, but I was the one guilty of giving him all my power, of becoming something that I was not just for the possibility of being able to escape my own private hell that I lived in.

The letter took him aback. Apparently, no one had been so "brutally honest" with him before, while at the same time expressing their gratitude to him for helping them to learn more about themselves. He did not like to be yelled at, thus the reason for the letter. I believe it was about seven or eight pages long. After reading it, we discussed it in detail. He asked me outright, "So you don't think that I can be the man that you need me to be?" My answer to him was that while he was a wonderful man, a perfect gentleman and a good catch, we were on opposite ends of the spectrum when it came to what my spirit needed.

I am affectionate all the time; he was uncomfortable (but getting used to) being affectionate. I am very uninhibited when it comes to sex; he was very "traditional." I am very in touch with and able to articulate my feelings; he was not. I am comfortable with stating my likes and dislikes and with asking for what I want; he was not comfortable with asking (I am not sure if he even knew what it was he wanted or if he did and was just afraid to ask for fear of not getting it). I had

The 5 Phases Of Dating

lived a very different adult life than he had. I had taken the time to work through my painful issues, memories from childhood; he was able to articulate his to a degree, but he held onto the old adage "that's just the way it's always been."

We were clearly from opposite ends of the spectrum and for me to continue to be true to my spirit, I had to face the fact that it just wasn't going to work. I could no longer be in that dating situation without getting the things that my spirit needed. While he was not the man for me, he was and still is a wonderful and caring person. If I was happy with someone giving me the world, showing me the world, but not sharing their spirit with me or their heart, then maybe it would have worked. However, deep down in my spirit, I know that I needed so much more than that. Money is great. Prestige is great. A big beautiful house in the suburbs is great. But what feeds my spirit goes so much deeper than material trinkets. And **that** my friends, he was unable to give me.

In the first two examples, I was seen as the "bad guy." I did not give in to what the other person wanted, whether it was to remain in Phase II or the demands of the other person wanting to see me "right now" to discuss our situation. In the third example, I can tell you that he never got angry with me for not continuing to date him. He never raised his voice or called me names. He never made me feel as though I was the bad guy. He was very concerned about his image, about how people remembered him. At the time, that is where we differed. I must admit, prior to that, I used to be the same way. Now, instead of always being the person to take the "high road" and not be completely honest because it might hurt someone's feelings or change the way they perceived me, I come from a place of honesty and integrity.

In each of these scenarios, I demonstrated what too many people are not known to give these days: the truth. I knew exactly where I was in my life and I was able to articulate that clearly. No amount of trying to convince me otherwise was going to change the truth of what I felt in my spirit as it related to each of these individuals.

Are they bad people? Absolutely not! Hell, the person in Example #2 and I have since gone on to work together with humanitarian efforts. She is a wonderful person with a huge heart. They were just not the right people for me to settle down with. They each had their own individual strengths, which is why I enjoyed hanging around with them to begin with. However, their personalities did not resonate within my spirit.

So, you see every person you encounter in the dating arena does not always turn out to be a relationship shoe-in. Each dating situation is an opportunity to learn more about yourself, your likes, dislikes, wants, needs, and desires, including the other person's quirks. The important thing is to be honest with yourself first. Know what you want and don't want. Have a damn good idea of what it is that will make your spirit sing and don't jump on the first train that pulls into your station. Remember, it might not be your train.

PHASE III: DATING EXCLUSIVELY - A COMMITTED RELATIONSHIP - LAYING THE FOUNDATION

Now that you have made the decision to date someone exclusively, let's talk about those spoken and unspoken expectations. The first thing we need to cover is the fact that you are in a *relationship*, not married. As you're moving into your relationship, you begin to lay the foundation for how the two of you will relate to one another. Therefore, there are certain things that you should not be expecting or allowing. They are as follows:

Answering the Phone or Door

What makes people think that once they have decided to date someone exclusively that he or she is entitled to answer that person's door or their phone? Unless you gave them permission to do so, whoever calls, texts, or rings your doorbell is none of their business.

If you did your homework up to this point, then you have a pretty good idea of who this person is, how they interact with their friends, how they feel about you, what your definitions of a relationship are and whether you're on the same page. If you have done your homework, then you are exempt from this section. However, if you are like me, and you make it a habit to read the entire book first then going back over it again with the highlighter and the notebook, then read on.

If you are still insecure about who is calling, wondering why they take certain phone calls and not others, or concerned that they make plans to be with some other person after you leave, then you have undoubtedly placed yourself in a relationship that is not based on trust or truth. I learned a lot from each of my past relationships, situationships and maintenanceships. Example number three taught me about the telephone. His philosophy was that if you are secure enough within your relationship, then it should not matter whether your mate answered the phone while you were sitting there, regardless to who it was. While you are the current person of choice, you are not the only person that he knows. The thing to concentrate on here is that you are privy to the conversation. How is he or she handling the conversation? Are they being disrespectful of you? Have you already shared with each other your concept of respect and disrespect?

If you have entered a relationship with this person and you cannot trust them to take a phone call or acknowledge your presence while on the phone, then why are you with them? Have you discussed this situation with him or her only to be ignored? Did they pay no heed to you prior to the decision to date exclusively? If so, why would you expect things to be different now?

Living Arrangements

This is another very important area. It is so common for those that are new in a relationship to slowly begin the move-in process. I once had a roommate that was like...well, let's just say a revolving door. Any guy she met at the club she would bring home with us. Several guys stayed for a few days at a time, and then were no longer seen; however, the last one was a different story.

He came home with us one night after a party as usual.

He stayed for the next three days. I firmly believed he had overstayed his welcome. However, he only left long enough to go and get fresh clothes. Without warning, he was living with us. When I asked her about it, she said he was only staying temporarily. "Temporarily" lasted until we ended up breaking the lease.

With this situation, the romance was hot and heavy. What appeared to be love, turned out to be two desperate people needing to be rescued. My roommate and "club guy" ultimately moved into a townhome together. He got custody of his daughter. They became pregnant, got married and divorced all within one and a half years. What a ride!!!

As a woman who longed to feel love as often as possible, I too have had my share of moving in entirely too soon. I have uprooted my children, changed their schools, and rearranged my home to include others' belongings. You name it; I've done it. Of course, I've done this while dating women. There's just something about the best friend aspect of dating a woman. You have a lot in common. You stay up late talking all night. You tend to want to reduce the stress level for your partner, whether it's the laundry, the cooking, or a financial factor.

Some of the common reasons (or shall we say proposed justifications) for initiating the living together arrangements are:
- Since we spend a lot of time together anyway, and your lease is up soon, why not just move in with me? It will save us both some money and allow us to have more disposable income;
- You'll be able to return to school;
- I just can't bare being without you. Why don't you

The 5 Phases Of Dating

stay here with me this week?
- Please don't go home; and
- You can stay here with me until you get on your feet, then if you want to move, you can. No strings attached.

A strong word of advice to you: keep your own place until you really get serious with someone. Convenience is not a good reason to move in together. Yes, it's cute and fun and "warm-n-fuzzy" in the beginning, but that will not last. You should be solid in your relationship, having experienced growing pains and overcoming communication hurdles prior to taking such a major step. It took my husband two years to get a set of keys to my condo when we were dating and it took us six years before we moved in with each other. When we did, we bought a house. If you are in financial trouble and you are looking for a convenient solution, then get a non-candidate, non-sexual roommate!

Just to reiterate, moving in too soon sets you up for the following emotional obstacles:
No longer feeling independent within your confines;
Having to abide by someone else's house rules;
- Walking around on eggshells trying not to upset the energy of the house;
- Not having your own 'sacred space' in your shared environment;
- Always wondering when the day will come when you will be "evicted";
- Having to kiss their ass depending on your financial situation;

- Changing their mind with respect to the expectations they have for you;
- Feeling as though you are a guest instead of feeling at home; and/or
- Having to adjust your sleep time, work time, time you spend with your friends to not upset the household.

The list can go on and on. The point is you need to get to know someone on neutral turf. You need a place to call your own, and so do they. You still need somewhere to go if you or the other person has a bad day, a bad attitude, or an alter ego. The worst feeling in the world is to be in a situation where you feel helpless, trapped, caught in a difficult situation, or like you have to kiss ass in order to have a place to live so that you can continue to receive someone's portion of the rent because you are dependent upon that money.

When there is no pressure to be nice, to keep the peace, to maintain a certain type of vibe, or to maintain a roof over your head, then you are free to be yourself. You can speak your mind. You can walk away from an unwanted, abusive, or volatile situation without having to get the police or your six brothers and his boys involved. You can tell a person to kiss **your** ass if necessary, and then go home to your own place, or send them home to theirs. You are not in a position to owe anybody anything, and from there you maintain your sense of independence and dignity.

Spend the time getting to know the other person without giving them too much freedom. Your place is your place. Decorate it the way you want. Light as many candles as you want. Play whatever type of music you want. Clean up whenever and however you want. You get the picture. Whether you choose to give them a key is up to you, but realize that you are giving this person access to your most private possessions: credit card information, family heirlooms, personal belongings, answering your phone, checking your caller id, etc. Do you know this person well enough to trust them with all that? Do you have a good idea of who they are and how trustworthy they are?

If there comes a time when you are serious about moving in together, then you should consider what that truly means. Talk about it in detail. Discuss what it would take for the two of you to feel comfortable with the new arrangement. Discuss everything from who does the cleaning, to how the bills should be handled. If you have the opportunity, why not make it a neutral new place that you both decide upon. This way the energy of "it still being the other person's place" won't hover over either of you. You can choose it together, choose the furniture, the décor, and identify your own space.

Communication

It is very important to maintain an open and honest line of communication. We are all changing every day, and as we change, items that you discussed and understood to be one way in the beginning may not be the same now. It is important to communicate the changes to your partner and to discuss them with each other once you discover them.

Relationships are like gardens for the cultivation and the

growth of your soul. When you enter an exclusive relationship with someone, you both expose yourselves to each other more than you did when you were only dating. As a result, you each serve as a gardener for the other. As with any garden, your mate will point out and uncover a few weeds. He will be the person to either point them out to you, or bring them out of you. This is not necessarily bad because without awareness, you would not have the opportunity to grow. Sometimes it takes someone close to point things out to you, showing you who you really are.

I hope that you have established a preferred way of communicating to each other so that you are able to receive this information in a way that is acceptable and non-threatening. However, please know that not all information will come to you in such a loving and well-thought out fashion. It does not mean that the information is not valid. Anything given to you as constructive criticism should be given careful thought before embracing it as valid. You could have a hard time accepting what you hear because no one has ever told you that before and you need a minute to sit and ponder. Alternatively, it could be this is not the first time that you have heard this. If that is the case then realize if more than three people have told you the same thing, it's highly likely that you need to take several seats and genuinely think about what it is they're saying about you. You might truly be surprised.

Accessing Email/Voicemail

I remember beginning one of my relationships without the element of trust. My partner was a social butterfly, very popular and had a flock of women waiting in the wings. In the

The 5 Phases Of Dating

beginning, this was a problem for me, which I made very clear. To make me feel more comfortable, trusting if you will, she offered me the passwords to her voicemail and her email so that I could check them anytime I felt unsure because she had nothing to hide. Sounds like a good idea, huh? **Not!**

This was not a good idea for several reasons:
1. It did not do anything for my sense of trust. I just assumed that she would create other email accounts that I did not know the password to and use that for her secrets.
2. It embarrassed me to know that she saw me for the insecure little "supposed to be strong" woman that I really was.
3. I battled constantly with whether I should check it.

Eventually I did check it. As they say, if you go looking for trouble, you will find it. Never again will I want the passwords to anyone's accounts. This was over twenty years ago. Passwords to phones or emails mean nothing to me. It's way too easy for someone to have multiple accounts, email, and social media to try and keep up with them. I have better things to do with my time than play Inspector Gadget trying to find something. Where there's a will, there's a way. I'd rather focus on being the type of woman that he can't imagine being without.

If you find yourself in a relationship where you feel the need to have password or access to everything that might allow that person to cheat on you, then you need to check (with) yourself. Should you even be in this relationship? It is never a good idea to commit to anything (whether it is a person, a job, a community organization, or a place of worship), where you don't feel comfortable or respected. Understand that it's not the other person's responsibility to make you feel secure or respected. Those feelings can come only from within. However, if you take the time to get to know who you are and identify what you are comfortable with, what is acceptable and what is not, then you stand a better chance of making the right choice based on your truth.

I knew walking into that relationship that I was not comfortable with the way she conducted herself, both inside and outside of a relationship; however, I went along with it anyway. For almost four years, I tortured myself and got angry because of behaviors that did not make me feel safe. I had gone against my spirit and what I knew was best for me. She did not, nor did she jump through any hoops to make a change. It was who she was, and she was very clear about living her **truth**. This relationship taught me a lot as well.

Stay True To You!

Once you enter a committed relationship, the rest of the world becomes less important to you. Everything you do is centered on the two of you as a couple. You start consulting with the other person first before you make any plans. You stop hanging out with your friends and use the excuse that you are still getting to know each other as the reason for the disconnection. Slowly you begin to stop doing things that you like to do to make time, just in case the other person wants to get together and do something...you know, just in case.

You need to be more careful not to lose sight of who

The 5 Phases Of Dating

you are as an individual. Yes, the newness of a relationship is wonderful; however, it is just a relationship. **It is not a marriage.** It is important for you to continue to do the things that you enjoy. You were an individual before you met this person and you need to continue to be one during your relationship. If you do not, then you risk smothering the other person or waking up one day and resenting that person because you no longer do the things that keep you grounded, the things that fed your spirit. Please understand that I am in no way stating that the institution of marriage automatically creates a restrictive and limited life experience; however, dating and being married are two very different situations.

In all honesty, it is not the other person's fault if you begin to stop living for the possibility of spending time with them. You are responsible for maintaining your own spiritual sanity. It is common to want to spend every waking moment together; however, you will appreciate the other person so much more (and your spirit will love you) if you don't lose sight of who you are. It is important for you to continue to grow as an individual so that you can continue to grow together. If you make sure that you are taking care of your own emotional and spiritual health, then that is one less stress factor you will be putting on your relationship. Remember, relationships are gardens for the soul, and they need constant weeding, watering, fertilizing, and nurturing. If you each take responsibility for your part of this garden, then it will make the relationship so much easier to maintain.

Anita M. Charlot

What's Yours Is Yours; what's Theirs Is Theirs

Just because you are in a relationship with someone does not mean you now have, as we would say in the Baptist Church, "All rights and privileges as any other member." A committed relationship does not give you automatic squatters' rights. Your money is your money. Your car is your car. Their home is their home. You are not automatically granted a key or joint ownership of anything. This is just a relationship.

Relationships come and go. They are not trial marriages. You are not granted automatic privileges. In sessions with my clients, I often come across women who feel slighted or cheated because of an entitlement theory. They have had their feelings hurt because they assumed being in a relationship with this person entitled them to everything.

They felt as though they had a say in what furniture or appliances to buy, what foods to eat, what color to paint the walls, and even how their partner spent their money. None of this has anything to do with you in the relationship phase. This relationship may not be the last one that you have before you marry; therefore, there is no entitlement. Maintain autonomy with your possessions and allow the other person to do the same. When the time comes, you will begin to make joint decisions and merge the households. Do not put the cart before the horse.

The 5 Phases Of Dating

Your Friends versus Our Friends

As you enter a relationship, you want your new love interest and your friends to all get along, right? Sometimes this can be challenging, especially if you and your ex have mutual friends. However, understand that even as a couple with a group of mutual friends it is still important to maintain your own individual set of friends as well.

With our own exclusive friends, we let our hair down. If you have true friends in your corner, this is where you can also turn to for advice on whether you were justified in your behavior, or if you are just being stubborn or out of control. Your true friends will be brutally honest with you one minute, yet love and respect whatever decision you make the next. They will not try to control you, but be an honest gauge as to whether your behavior is selfish or off the charts.

Do you and your mate a favor: have your own set of friends and allow your partner to have his or her own set, but also try to have some common friends that are couples as well, preferably those that have healthy relationships you both can learn from. Who wants to spend social time around miserable people? Misery loves company, and if your friends are not happy in their relationships, there is no way in hell they can be genuinely happy for you in yours, and they cannot provide sound advice or make supportive suggestions to you.

Flipping the Script

There have been a number of clients who behaved

one way in the beginning in order to gain the attention, attraction and even love of a man and then later "flipped the script" and became someone different. In those cases, these women felt that since they had already laid the foundation so to speak, that they could then relax? And why wouldn't they, since they had already done all the hard work. They had done things like:

- Wooed the individual;
- Kept off those pounds;
- Sexed them to death;
- Listened to all their boring stories;
- Gave up all your personal time;
- Laughed at all their dumb-ass jokes;
- Made them feel comfortable with you;
- Won their heart over;
- Presented yourself to be the perfect person for them;
- Talked the necessary game;
- Pretended their thoughts and feelings really mattered to you; and
- Pretended their way of communicating is something that you've always wanted.

Once they accomplished these things, they felt as though they could take a break. They felt since they already had the man and that they had won his heart, the thought that it was ok to:

- Let those extra pounds hang around a little longer;
- Stop watching what you eat;

The 5 Phases Of Dating

- Just say whatever is on your mind;
- Not be intimate with them if you don't feel like it;
- Not have time for their stories;
- Start spending time alone;
- Relax and let your true self come out;
- Change everything about yourself and expect them to continue to be with you because they love you now;
- Cut them off midsentence because you are tired of them talking, yet come back later and expect them to willingly to listen to you intently and completely; or
- Tune out what they're saying because they now remind you of something or someone else.

Or, they stopped doing the following:
- Sharing their feelings;
- Cooking them dinner like they used to;
- Make love to them as often (or as good) as in the past;
- Keep doing the nice things that they used to;
- Put their needs and desires first;
- Make time to listen to their stories;
- Be as understanding as they were in the beginning; or
- Working on their own personal growth.

Do you think this type of behavior is going to keep the relationship going? Absolutely not! Becoming content in a relationship is a recipe for losing the relationship.

This is why so many relationships never make it to

Phase IV. Just because you were the chosen one doesn't mean that you get to let yourself go. The very thing you did to win this person is what needs to continue to keep this person, plus a little extra. As time goes on, you will each grow individually, and if you work at it, collectively as well. You will relax into the relationship and things that you never knew were an issue before will surface. Other things that you thought were no longer an issue will pop up yet again. Instead of being defensive and inconsiderate about the other person's feelings, you should sit down and try to understand where the person is coming from. Remember the spiritual garden analogy: you need to weed, water, and plant new seeds. Sprinkle fertilizer, nurture and protect your relationship; otherwise, you are going to lose it to neglect.

Here's another relationship analogy-Purchasing a new car

When you purchase a car, you are all excited. You want to get in and drive it as often as you can. You want to show it off to your friends, family, exes, hell...anybody. You keep it clean inside and out. You dare not even curse in the car or have heated conversations on your cell phone. You spray Money Blessings spray as your air freshener and even hang the crystal from with rear view mirror to catch all the negativity from the cars around you.

You dare not eat or allow others to smoke in or close to it. It's as though you have such a high regard for this car. Hell, I would even go as far as to say you **respect** it. Who would have thought **you** would be driving **this** car? This is the best thing since sliced bread and you even have cute pet names for it. You would not think of being inconsiderate and allowing the gas

The 5 Phases Of Dating

tank to go beyond half-full, letting the windows remain dirty or not keeping the interior free of trash. If you hear a knock or a rattle, you quickly investigate. Of course, why wouldn't you? You want to make sure that everything is okay, that she does not need any special attention from the mechanic. And if it is determined that she does, you make it your business to take care of it almost immediately.

As time goes on and you become more comfortable and accustomed to it, guess what happens? The newness wears off! It starts by letting the car get a little dirty, then it graduates to the point of the dirt changing the color of the car altogether. The tank gets down to 1/4 full before you make it to the gas station, that is if you don't wait until the car signals that it needs gas by turning on that cute little gas pump light. You have gone from not eating in your car to there being more French fries between the seats than in the McDonald's bag. The sweet talk to the car stops, and you begin to treat the car like you would treat anybody else. The crystal hanging from the rear-view mirror now gets on your nerves, as it sways back and forth. Road rage has returned. You now curse at the other cars in front of you. The floors have not been vacuumed in weeks. You have not taken care of the regular maintenance on the car, and then you start to hear noises. You let it go because it would be an inconvenience for you to take the car in for a checkup, and then you wonder what is wrong with it. Of course, it cannot be breaking down, not after **all** you've done in the past!

Then it stops working one day. You curse the car, blame the manufacturer, blame your mate for driving it, and blame the gas at the gas stations. You blame everything and everybody but yourself. Surely, it cannot be your fault! But who is to blame here? I'll tell you, if you haven't figured it out yet: **you are**! How could you expect it to run the same, get good mileage, and remain looking new when you haven't taken care of it? You did not tend to its basic needs. You did not do all the things that you were doing in the beginning to keep it healthy. Can you see where I am going here?

Relationships are the same.

The very thing you did in the beginning to get that person, is what you will need to continue to do (either that, or something better) to keep them. **Commitment does not equal contentment.** Let me repeat that one a little louder for you, **COMMITMENT DOES NOT EQUAL CONTENTMENT!**

Relationships need nurturing, regular maintenance, and care just as your car does. Would you expect your car to be dependable if you do not take care of it? How can you expect your mate to be dependable if you are not nurturing and taking care of your relationship? If you are not the person you were in the beginning, how can you expect them to be the same person they were? Things change. People change, and tolerance levels change. If your relationship really means something to you, nurture it now before it disintegrates. And don't have the audacity to wonder why people cheat. If you don't want your mate looking elsewhere for the things that feed their spirit, make sure that they are well fed within your relationship. What you are not willing to do, believe me, someone else will.

The 5 Phases Of Dating

Advance or Retreat

Let's say that after some time in your relationship, you have determined because of your mate coming completely out of several proverbial bags on you and letting the real person show, that you are not getting your basic needs met. What do you do? Do you go out and find someone that will feed those needs? Of course, they'll be easy to find and more than willing to accommodate you, as they want to distract you from your current situation. Or do you communicate your feelings to your mate and try to work together on resolving them? Naturally, it's ideal and recommended to choose the latter; however, due to filters and defense mechanisms that block effective communication, this may be a task that may be too big for the two of you.

Always remember that **you** are the most important person. You should never continue to remain in any type of relationship where you are consistently putting your needs on the back burner to keep the peace. You deserve to be happy, respected, understood, validated, honored, and adored, just like the other person. I lived most of my adult life through my first marriage and countless relationships, putting the needs of others before my own. This was a pattern for me. I felt that if I acquiesced to their needs, then they would one day return the favor. That did not happen. It doesn't work that way. If a person is unable to hear you due to their filters or their defense mechanisms, no amount of drama, crying, pleading, bargaining, or throwing yourself onto the sword is going to change that.

You need to consider the relationship very carefully. Is

this something that the two of you can work out? Do you need to accept the reality of the situation and recognize that this person is unable to give you what you need? Do you have someone else in your life to confide in, someone who validates you? Is your mate trying to grow in this area? Is the relationship important enough for you to continue to work on rebuilding, while simultaneously allowing space for you and your mate to become better people, individually as well as part of your relationship?

Do not sit around waiting for the day when they will be able to do the things you want or be that chosen one for you. Recognize that somewhere in your immediate surroundings there may be a person who currently possesses those spirit-filling qualities for you. And if that is not the case, there's nothing wrong with seeking them out. A while back, I realized that the very things I gave in my relationships (both intimate and platonic), I did not receive in return. While this was a sad realization, I recognized that it did me no good to sit around and sulk about it. Resenting people for not being who I wanted or needed them to be was not going to make them turn into that person any faster. Having to beg for something or feel as though I had to fight for something did not provide the same inner peace once I received it. It was always overshadowed by the fact that it was not given freely, but only after needing to perform some major arm twisting.

Take Care Of You!

So, what was a girl to do? Well, being a member of the helping profession, I decided to seek help to enable me

The 5 Phases Of Dating

to get in touch with my own feelings, while I assisted others in getting in touch with theirs. I knew exactly the type of person that I wanted, so I diligently put that description out into the Universe. Shortly afterwards, I found her. She came with all the credentials that I wanted: a student and practitioner of metaphysics for over twenty years with professional training in psychology and philosophy, a good spirit, and a "right between the eye" coaching style like that of mine with my clients.

We hit it off immediately from the very first telephone conversation. It turned out that she had followed the same path that I had metaphysically. She shared with me her life's experiences just as I share mine with my clients. She could automatically speak to the challenges that I was facing just as I am able to with my clients, and she had a sense of humor. What more could I ask for? Having found her and knowing that at least twice a month I would have "Anita-only" time, where I could explore everything that I didn't feel safe in sharing with friends or family was beneficial. Here in this safe space that I created for myself, I felt validated, understood, honored, listened to, challenged, and called to. Granted, I was paying for it, but it was just what I needed.

How did it affect my involvement in my relationships with others? Well for starters, it gave me a true **reality check**. It also removed the stress that I was placing on my mate to be everything that I needed, thus ending my disappointment and resentment. I finally had a safe place. In that haven, I learned so many things about myself and about my interactions with people, both from the past and in the present. Hell, I even began to cultivate a complete picture of what I wanted the future to look like. I vowed at that time that I would never walk this earth again without having a space for me, and only me in my home environment. Whether I had it in any relationship, or I had to pay for it out of pocket, I would have my space because it allowed me to continue to get in touch with the reality of who I was and started me on the lifelong journey of sharing these findings with women just like you.

PHASE IV: ENGAGEMENT- PLANNING A LIFE TOGETHER - BUILDING THE HOUSE

Congratulations! You have made it this far without putting the book down. Not as "finger-pointing" as you thought it would be, huh? We are now only beginning to build the house. You thought you'd experienced enough hard work up to this point.

Healthy relationships of any kind will require different levels of work. Just like growing or cultivating a garden and taking care of a car, there will always be weeds to pull or maintenance checks. So is the same with relationships. Now that you have made that long-term commitment to each other, there is next level work to do to prepare for that life together. Certain things need to be and should be addressed prior to making that final step. Remember you are building on a promise to spend the rest of your days, not just nights, with this person, and that could mean an entirely different set of issues than just being in a relationship.

R-E-S-P-E-C-T Your Relationship

Have you ever run across a situation where no matter how many times you explained to your mother that "this is the person" for you, she continues to talk about them as though they are the flavor of the month? She constantly reminds you that your last boyfriend was a good person. "When was the last time you talked to so and so?" Or what about that friend who is constantly trying to "hook you up" with someone because they don't like the person that you're dating, or better yet, are now engaged to? How do you handle that?

The 5 Phases Of Dating

Most of us have encountered someone that refused to respect the sanctity of our relationship, whether it was a friend, an ex, an admirer, or a family member. They continue to say disrespectful things to you and try to convince you to go out and do things they would not do (or are doing) to disrespect your relationship. They may also keep bringing up the past and what could have/should have been. They keep making inappropriate comments about what they would do to you/for you if they were your mate.

Hopefully you are not allowing yourself to be lured away by these relationship leeches. But just in case you have been, let me point out the typical behavioral patterns for these personality types:

- The more you continue to allow them to do it, the more they will.
- If you tell them to stop and they do not, yet you continue to interact with them, then you are telling them that it is okay to disrespect you and your relationship.
- If they are promising you the world and painting pretty pictures for you, then you can guarantee that after they have managed to break up your current relationship and get you over to their side, they will change.

Here is a classic case of what happens when you allow others to disrespect your relationship:

A man begins a "secret friendship" outside of your relationship with another woman that is clearly interested in him. To make matters worse, this woman is already in a relationship. When it becomes known that he has had a friendship with this woman unbeknownst to you and her man, you ask questions like, *If it is purely plutonic then why doesn't her man know about it? Why can't we all be friends and hang out as couples?* Now your questions are met with finger pointing and accusations that you are too insecure, and that there is nothing for you to be tripping about. He might say, *you're being silly. There you go again with that jealousy stuff. She is a nice person and I like talking to her. You can't tell me who to have as a friend.* Women know women, and we know all too well how this will play out.

So, you try to explain that their intentions are not pure. If the friendship had to be a secret, then there was more to it, whether they acted on it or not. Since you have been with him for some time now, you start second-guessing yourself. You think, *maybe I am being silly. I should trust him more. I'm tripping.* You tell yourself whatever you need to in an attempt to not anger him or appear to be weak. You believe his BS yet again and take all the weight of this drama inside. You stop asking questions, even though you notice things more every day, but you don't say anything to keep the peace.

This continues for a while, as the two of you grow more distant from each other. You stop connecting with your friends and family because they warned you. They may have even shared sightings of him out in public with her, and now you're embarrassed and ashamed. This is normal Love, it happens more often than you think. You are not the only one here, and you do not have to put up with this.

No amount of sex, empty promises or lavish lifestyle is worth you settling for a man that is not even able, capable, or

The 5 Phases Of Dating

willing to respect the sanctity of the commitment that he made to you. If he is being this disrespectful before you walk down the aisle, I'd hate to see what happens after you are formally and legally bound to him. Continuing to put up with this and other disrespectful acts is not the way you show love or commitment to your man. Doing this sends a completely different message, the message that you do not love yourself enough to expect respect from him. If you marry him, then you are looking at a life filled with more disrespectful moments. Loving yourself and respecting yourself first is key. And if you happen to find yourself in this position, remember that he is not the last man to love you or the last man on earth. However, he should be the last man that is allowed to treat you less than what you need, want, and deserve. I can believe it all day for you, but **you** must believe it for yourself.

As a grown-ass woman, I need you to stop pointing fingers at the men in your life and start taking responsibility for your actions or inactions as needed. This is the only way for you to attract and maintain an authentic relationship by being authentic with yourself. Having said that, let's think about this scenario a little more. What would be the draw for him? How could she capture his attention? You live with him, so when does he have time to talk to her? Where there is a will there is a way. The idea here is not for me to blame you for his indiscretions or make you feel even more insecure or suspicious if you already do, but rather to point a few things out to you in case these things have never crossed your mind before. I've interviewed plenty of men in my years, and even though my target market is women, I've also coached single and married men who were more than willing to share with me **why** they tend to look in a different direction.

All men look in a different direction! Yes, I said it. They **all** look in a different direction; however, based on their emotional maturity and their connection to the women in their lives, they make the choice whether to walk in a different direction. What types of things do you think would make a man look in a different direction? Most women would say it's due to the man's:

- age;
- lack of maturity;
- inability to keep his penis in his pants;
- high sex drive;
- want for variety;
- need to conquer as much as he can;
- desire to keep up with his single friends; or
- running away from his problems or responsibilities.

What if I told you that while those things are true, there is an entirely different list that you may not have ever considered? As women, we grow up with a fairy tale idea of who a man should be in our lives and based on our familial history, our relational experience, and the women that we surround ourselves with, this could be a very distorted view of the truth. As a result, we never really learned to understand men's spirits and their emotional needs. Not to mention when a man shows any sign of emotion, he is considered either weak, or possibly gay. Just as there are different types of women with different types of personalities, the same applies to men. Many men that have crossed my path have cited these characteristics of women, who

The 5 Phases Of Dating

have caught their attention. She is a woman who is the following:

- confident;
- attractive;
- nurturing; or
- comfortable in her body, no matter what size she is.
- She also does the following:
- doesn't have a history with him;
- makes him feel appreciated;
- listens to him complain about you (whether all truth or not) and strokes his ego;
- makes him feel desired; and/or
- makes him feel needed.

Have you ever considered these things? Did you know that men can be just as emotional as women? This is where the disconnect is. Men do not always act on their attraction to another woman; however, the reasons for his attraction are often not what we would expect. Am I telling you that it is your responsibility to keep your man's eyes from wandering? Yes and no. What I am saying is that the more you tap into the spirit of the man, the less likely it is that he will want to act upon his wandering eye. And let's be honest here ladies, we look at other men just as often as they look at other women. We are just a lot more discrete about it. Time to own your *ish as a grown-ass woman and get in touch with the truth of **you** first before looking to a man to do it for you.

So how do you respond to the advances of another man

while respecting your relationship? You do so by thanking him for his interest and letting him know that you are already in engaged. Here are a few examples of responses I've given in the past:

- In response to a request for my phone number; I don't think my boyfriend, fiancé, husband would appreciate that.
- In response for an innocent coffee date; Thank you, that's very nice of you to offer but I wouldn't want my husband going on innocent coffee dates so I think I'll pass.
- In response to a man trying to pay for my coffee or my drink at the counter: No thank you, that's very nice of you but my husband makes sure I have more than enough to take care of my wants and my needs.

"Deceptive Advertising 2.0"

My mother always told me, "Don't start something you don't plan on continuing." This idiom included relationships, friendships, as well as on the job activities. If you start the relationship off by cooking them dinner every Friday, unless you are going to do that for the remainder of the relationship, don't start. If you start the relationship by allowing them to bring their laundry over, you wash it, fold it, then deliver it back to them, then don't get angry when they look to you to do the laundry later as well. Or be very clear about the fact that it may change as time goes on. This way you are not setting yourself up to be criticized for pretending to be something that you aren't if you so choose to reduce or eventually stop this activity.

This is another reason it is a good idea to take your time in dating and getting to know a person before making a formal commitment. If you take your time, you will see how, in time, things change and you and your partner can discuss them rationally, and recognize whether the change is something you can deal with long term. Patience and taking things slow is beneficial for both parties. And once you get in touch with your **truth**, you will then have a better idea of what you will and will not be open to continuing. It is important to articulate those things up front and have the courage to openly discuss anything that changes during the relationship with ease. If you started off thinking that you would be okay with doing all the driving, cooking, and cleaning, but that changes, talk about it. If you tolerated certain comments or behaviors in the beginning that are now negatively affecting you, then talk about them.

Living Arrangements

Once you become engaged and begin planning a life together, the idea of living together will come up. However, that doesn't mean that you should rush into it. There are many things to consider. For example:

- Inventory of property: What is considered extra and what to do with those extras?
- If one of you is renting, should you wait until the lease is up or sublet your apartment?

- If both of you own property, will you keep both and rent one out, or will you sell both and buy a larger place together?
- Distance between living locations and your places of employment: How many additional tolls, miles, or oil changes will be added to your commute?
- If you are between residences, how will the utilities be split? What will be your contribution to the combined household considering you are still financially responsible for your place?

All these things and many more should be discussed in detail **before** either of you move in. I have witnessed the arguments, resentments, and misunderstandings that arise due to the lack of clarity in these areas, even if you have been in your relationship for many years. Things that you managed to overlook or accept as "just the way they are" will begin to bother you as you consider combining households.

Your Junk...My Junk

I remember feeling as though my personal household items were junk that didn't matter. Of course, this was never stated to me; however, my things were resting frigidly in the garage, while theirs were nice and toasty in the house. Not to mention dusty because they had not been used, touched, or even thought about for months, maybe even years, before I moved in. I would find myself battling the heat and cold trying to locate that one item I needed, which was somewhere in a box

The 5 Phases Of Dating

in the garage. At first, it didn't matter because everything inside the house had its place. And my stuff was just extra. I didn't need it immediately, so I was okay with it being stored in the garage.

Then as time went on, I noticed how much of my stuff was packed away in boxes, and how much of her stuff, that wasn't being used, was just sitting around collecting dust. In my effort to keep from disturbing the household energy, I didn't say anything. I wanted her to recognize the inconvenience that I had to endure just to gain access to something. So, I waited and waited and waited for what seemed like eternity, silently harboring more and more resentment.

One day during a discussion of something else that I felt to be unfair and inconsiderate, I brought up the "junk" issue. I mentioned how I felt as though her things were more important than mine. I told her how I felt as though I was renting a room with a huge storage space in the garage. I shared with her how it unnerved me to have to go outside, during the winter getting fully dressed, to have access to my things. I mentioned several different areas in the house where the dust was collecting quite a bit and how **those** things should be in the garage and mine should come inside.

She told me she had no idea that I felt that way, and she hadn't even thought about it. She asked me to point out which areas I wanted to move my things to and she would go through and clear those areas out so that the feeling of me and my things being spread out between the house and the garage would dissolve. Because of this discussion, she did whatever I asked, moved whatever, and assisted me in whatever way necessary for me to feel as though my personal belongings were just as valuable to her as they were to me. The key was talking about it. Once the resentment and the territorial issues were off the table, we both realized that we had an ample amount of junk and decided in our own time and in our own way how to get rid of it.

Continue To Feed Your Spirit

The quickest way to bring tension into any relationship is by not continuing to do activities that make you feel good. It is very important that you nurture and continue to nurture your spirit within your relationship, for if you don't, you'll find yourself becoming resentful of your partner. As in all new relationships, we tend to make the new person our world. Nothing else is as important. Slowly we stop participating in things as individuals that makes us feel alive. For me those things include spending an entire day at my favorite bookstore, with absolutely no distractions, walking through the park barefoot, lying in the grass, going for long walks in beautiful serene surroundings, sharing metaphysical concepts with open-minded individuals, and a host of other things.

What feeds your spirit? What have you moved so far away from that it seems like a thing of the past? Can you sit down and recall a day, time, or incident that made you feel as though you were on top of the world? What happened to that feeling, that incident? When was the last time you allowed yourself to have that feeling again? Why are you depriving yourself of the very thing that will keep you grounded? If you don't continue to feed your spirit, then you will lose touch with

The 5 Phases Of Dating

it. You will consistently feel alone even in your relationship. You will notice every little thing about your partner, like what they are and are not doing, or how they continue to put their needs, wants, and desires first.

Of course, the easiest thing to do would be to blame your partner, or to call them inconsiderate/insensitive. Perhaps, you might state that it always seems to be about them, and ask when is it going to be **your** turn?

Let me give you a bit of advice here: when you continue to nurture your spirit, make time for yourself, take your **own** turn, then you can't blame your mate for not pushing you to do so. Happiness comes from within, and there is no one on this earth that knows what will make us happy at any given moment but ourselves. If you continue to put your relationship first and yourself second, then you cannot point a finger at someone else. If you find that you have disconnected from the things that truly make you happy and feed your spirit, then it's time you got back to it. Grab your journal, make a list of what you haven't done in a long time or what you have always wanted to do, and then commit to doing at least one activity per week. Sign up for that class. Take that trip. Paint that picture. Learn that skill. Do whatever you need to do to love on you so that you have more love to give to others. It's impossible to give to others what you have not yet learned to give to yourself. If you don't, then you must face the fact that **you** are the reason why you have become disconnected from your spirit and stop blaming others.

Anita M. Charlot

The Balancing Act of Compromise

To compromise means to make a concession or give up something that is important to you for the sake of the other person or to reach a happy medium. It is important that your relationship does this in a healthy way. You may need to step outside of your comfort zone to try something new; a new dish, a new country, a new outfit, etc. these are all things that will stretch you but will also add to the richness of your relationship just for having indulged your partners desire to do something different.

Too much compromise from one person in the relationship will put stress on your connection to each other.

To compromise on what movie to watch, whether you have chicken or fish for dinner or where to place the furniture in your home are easy choices and often quite manageable. On the other hand, if one person begins to give up too much of their or important in a relationship as long as it does not mean that you are consistently doesn't always mean that the person in the relationship gets what they want. Sometimes everyone benefits, and other times only one-person benefits; however, in the game of love, no one feels as if their wants and needs are being ignored. Many times, I have forgotten about what was important to me to maintain what was important to my relationships, including relationships with family, friends, and exes. I thought I was compromising and being the best person, I could be, but what I was really doing was conceding. It is not compromise when you give more of your energy,

The 5 Phases Of Dating

understanding, and compassion than you are getting. It is not compromise when you put the feelings of your mate before your own all the time. It's not compromise when you stay in a friendship, relationship, or marriage where you are consistently being mentally, verbally, emotionally, physically, or spiritually abused. It's not compromise when you take a step back to allow the other person to have control when deep down inside it's tearing you apart. It's not compromise when you pretend to be okay with a certain behavior, attitude, or area of control when it doesn't make you feel good, loved, or appreciated.

Compromise brings about a solution where everyone benefits. One partner should not feel as though they must concede to maintain peace. Nor should one partner always end up being the person to be placed in a position to have to compromise. Relationships and marriages are balancing acts; both partners need to equally feel as though they are being respected, validated, and understood in a variety of ways. Throughout the course of your relationship, and marriage for that matter, there will be times when the two of you will develop a solution useful for both of you, and there will also be times when you will sit down and come to a conclusion that will benefit one person, but not the other. Here are a few examples of compromise:

- One person works full time while the other person works part time and finishes school.
- One person works close to daycare so that the kids get picked up on time.
- He goes to see a "chick flick" with you and you go see an action movie with him.

- He watches the kids while you go out with the girls.
- You don't complain when he goes to hang out with the boys vs. go to your nieces 6-year old birthday party.
- A few examples of conceding are:
- One person never gets to do the things they want to do.
- One wants to go to Disneyland with the kids, the other person insists that they go back to the same vacation spot as last year even though Disney is cheaper and they go without speaking up.

Being Supportive Versus Being Overbearing

How many of you have found yourselves in situations where you felt you knew exactly what your mate **should** do and didn't hesitate to deliver your opinion? Is this healthy? Should you or should you not speak up in areas where you see your partner being take advantage of? Do you feel that now, because you all are engaged, that you have the **right** to say whatever you want to say? Actually, you don't.

Telling things, the way you see it is fine, even giving advice is fine. The problem comes when you automatically assume that your way is the right way (the best way to handle "their" situation) or you're trying to *Keep it 100*. I have learned throughout the years the importance of knowing exactly what your mate needs from you when they say they need to talk. A former boss once said to me, "I trust you to make the right choices. If you find at any time that you need to talk to me about something, feel free to come into my office or grab me on my

The 5 Phases Of Dating

way past your desk. All I ask of you is that you tell me what hat to wear. If you want me to tell you what to do, let me know that. If you just want me to listen, while you think out loud, tell me that too. And if you want me to listen to your ideas and coach you in making the decision that **you** feel is best, then tell me that as well. I don't want you to come in here needing one thing from me and leaving feeling unsatisfied or disrespected at all."

I found that this approach not only works in corporate America, but also in your relationships. The same goes for your partnership. Yes, you are building a life together; however, you are not the person's mother, boss, or guru of their situations. If you got with them because you saw their potential and figured that you could change them or help them to be better even if they couldn't see it, then you entered the relationship for the wrong reasons.

Let me put it this way. If you continue to see the person as someone that you have to fix, teach, or tell what to do, then you will lose respect for them and they will become annoying and unattractive to you. When they approach you sensually, it will make your skin crawl. You will begin to pick apart everything that they say and everything they do because you have put them in a different position. Instead of seeing the person and treating them like your partner, you have started treating them like your child or student of your life class.

If it's a man we're discussing, then you will begin to emasculate him, and he will lose his drive to lead. If you continue to take over or take the lead, then don't get mad when you want him to step up, and he doesn't do it. Each time he tries to step up and take the lead and you complain about how you would have done it differently, he will eventually stop having an independent thought of his own and will continually look to you to make the final decision, so you can't blame him when it doesn't work out. Allow your man to **be** the man and learn how to encourage the leader in him to come out.

If you don't like raising your men, then stop attracting men who need to be raised. Allow him to take the lead, to make a mistake, and to know that it is okay for him to do so. The more you encourage him to lead, the more he will want to do it to make you continuously proud of him.

What if you are a woman that is used to being in charge at the office? What if it is killing you to watch him take the long way to complete something or to do it completely different than you would have? What then? How do you deal with this?

Understand that we each make decisions based on numerous factors. On the surface, it may appear as though we are making a decision in favor of the other person; however, the truth is everything we do, we do as a measure of protection for us.

For example, the girlfriend of a single father may feel that he is too lenient with his son's mother when it comes to certain responsibilities. She may offer her opinion on what she thinks would be the right way to handle things, yet she cannot understand why he insists on doing it his way.

What she assumed as the father allowing leniency may be him choosing which battles he would fight and how. Behind choosing those battles could be a long history of drama between him and his child's mother that he managed to keep at bay to maintain a cordial relationship with her. Certain fights would bring that drama back to the forefront and upset the calm he had created. What he needed was not for her to pass judgment

The 5 Phases Of Dating

on him for not doing things the way she thought he should do them, but for her to understand that he had his reasons. If choosing which battles to fight had no direct effect on their relationship or the welfare of his children, then it was his choice to make. As this couple continues to grow closer and plan their life together, there are different ways to address this issue without being overbearing.

Holding the assumption that he was protecting her was not only incorrect, but it also gave him no credit for being an individual with the capacity to make up his own mind. This could cause him to feel as though he was in the middle of the woman he loved and the mother of his child. Pushing the issue before it's time would make him feel as though he had to choose between his child or her. Any good father would choose his child.

Hopefully by the time the two of you are planning a life together, you have already found a way to have this conversation and have respectfully come up with a compromise that is comfortable for both of you. If he always must be on defense when you do not agree with his choices, and you do so in a way that rubs him the wrong way, you run the risk of him shutting down on you. Because of the way she handles this situation, it could result in him not sharing or talking to her about anything. Please don't think for one moment that because you are building a life together that you know everything or will ever understand or agree for that matter on everything, You won't. The fastest way to draw a wedge between you and your mate is to be controlling, judgmental, or attacking.

Your mate should feel safe to be exactly who he is. He should feel comfortable honestly discussing his feelings with you without fearing your judgment and condemnation, or emotional or physical retaliation. This type of behavior is precisely what causes individuals to stray from their relationships. If your mate feels misunderstood or judged, as though they can't do anything right, or if they feel ridiculed, shamed, or left alone to fend for themselves in a stressful situation, then they are a prime target for the next person (other woman) to come along and give them the very things that you are not. Would you leave your child in the hands of someone that was verbally and mentally abusive? Then why would you expect your mate to stick around and be treated in this way?

PHASE V: MARRIAGE OR LIFETIME COMMITMENT - LEARNING, LOVING, AND GROWING TOGETHER

Congratulations!

Having been married and divorced and married again, I applaud you for having made it thus far in your relationship. Marriage is not for everyone, so while I use the word marriage, this section also applies to those that have made a lifetime commitment to each other. Either way you look at it, it's not for the faint at heart. However, if you have been successful in determining your wants, needs and desires prior to this point, you should have all the preliminary relationship mechanics worked out already. All that's needed now is a combined sense of partnership, open communication, and the willingness to be vulnerable in a safe environment.

Communication

This is one area where you will continue to grow and stretch. So many times couples hold onto what they consider to be "little indiscretions" that they begin to shut down and hold things inside. They make comments to the other like, *What's the point? He's not going to understand me anyway. She never acknowledges my feelings. I may as well be talking to a wall. She tunes me out. He should have known that comment would hurt my feelings, because we've been together so long.*

It doesn't matter how long you have been together, each of you is continuously changing. You are growing mentally, physically, and spiritually. You are never the same person at any given moment. The cells in your body are constantly creating, dying, and regenerating. Your thoughts are bombarding you daily. Your feelings are aroused at different times for varied reasons. As you read, watch television or a

The 5 Phases Of Dating

movie, converse with other people, or witness something happening to someone you know, your values, opinions, and ideals change. Now if all of this is taking place, how on earth can you expect to know your partner or for your partner to know who you are and what you're thinking at any given moment? It's not possible.

As crazy as that may sound, many relationships are broken due to the lack of communication. We seem to think that if we decide to change our mind or our view on an issue, then we are wrong and we run the risk of losing the love and respect of our partner. If you are open with your partner and the two of you share conversations about more than just bills, sex, and children, then you should feel safe in sharing your internal changes with your mate. There is nothing like being in a marriage with someone and not being able to be completely vulnerable or be accepted for being 100% of who you are.

Pick a day/evening during the week to do nothing but communicate. Whether it's talking about your weekly activities or discussing changes that you have made and/or have noticed in the other person. Communicate. Communicate. Communicate! And be sure not to use this time to be defensive or to point a finger. This needs to be a time that is safe, sacred, and scheduled. You should use your first scheduled time to set up the boundaries of the meetings.

And never...ever...**ever** make a major decision while your hormones are raging!

Anita M. Charlot

Choosing Your Battles

During your marriage there will be plenty of times where you would like to interject smart comments into your conversations with your mate, or where you want to scold your partner for something they did differently than you. You may want to fight to maintain your position. Let's say that you do *all* these things. Was it necessary? Did you have to speak up in all scenarios? If so, why?
Do you like putting tiny little holes in your partner's heart? Do you prefer to make withdrawals from your love account instead of making deposits? Do you enjoy being on top, in control, in charge, or right all the time? Would you rather be right or happy?
Seriously. Ask yourself the last question if you find yourself to be this personality type.
I point this out to my clients all the time. I respond in our sessions with comments such as, "And yelling and screaming about how your mate doesn't do the dishes exactly the way you've done them all your life is truly going to encourage them to do them again, right? Now that you have had time to cool off from your argument, was it worth instructing your partner on how to do something when their way was working fine for them, *and* it was **still** getting done?"
Choose your battles. Life, love, and living a life together is hard enough without adding additional stress and strain to it. Encourage your partner's wacky way of doing things. Don't point out their faults. If it is still going to have the same result and not cause anyone to lose any body parts in the process, then let them do it their way. One thing I can point out here is when the moment arrives where I feel as though I am being micro-

managed, I shut down. If you want it done **that** particular way, *and* you are going to come behind me and correct my "mistakes," then **do it yourself damn it**! You will save us the extra work, grief, and resentment.

My suggestion to you is this: when you find yourself getting irritated about your partner doing anything differently than the way you do it, just stop and think for a moment. If we have an argument over this topic, will that negative energy do anything to strengthen our marriage or tear it down? Let go of the perfectionist attitude and learn to co-exist in this new world that the two of you are creating together.

Improve Each Other

Make sure that you continuously do things together that will allow you both to live the quality of life that you desire. Sit down and begin to create your Purrfect Life Story since you have found your mate for life. Construct your story together based on what your combined quality of life issues will be, and set goals to live that life. If it means setting aside a weekend at your favorite Bed and Breakfast, then call and make the reservation. Just do it. The family that has the same vision will continue to grow together.

Everyone Else...Butt Out!!!

Friends, family, and coworkers have no place in your marriage. I have heard plenty of my coworkers come to work and use the lunchroom as their therapy office. The 12 o'clock crowd is not qualified to give you advice on your mate. Listen to them if you want to and watch how much tension is stirred up at home. There are those rare occasions when the advice that you received during lunchtime may help to spruce up your love life; however, my experience is that the conversations are usually gripe sessions about what someone didn't do, don't do, won't do, and what they can do about it.

I've heard the LTL's (lunch time lawyers) give all types of advice on child support, how to catch your man cheating, and how to be the other woman. It is **amazing** what people will bring to their coworkers about their personal lives. I have always tried to be the type of person to take my lunch separate from the LTL crowd as often as possible. Even with the best intentions, it's hard not to listen in on the gossip. Furthermore, what makes people think that their coworkers are not looking at them differently because they know their business? As hard as I try, I can't help it.

Why would you want to bring your problems to your place of employment anyway? You never know the intention behind the comments of the LTL committee. Don't trust your marriage to people that consider their lives to be up for discussion during the commercial breaks of *All My Children* in the lunchroom. Just because they are willing to air their dirty laundry at the office doesn't mean that you should also. That goes for friends and family too; consider the source. If you know that your sister can't seem to keep a husband (or boyfriend for that matter) to save her life, then why would you talk to her about yours? If your mother has been married four times, why would you give her the privilege of free speech with regards to your marriage? Use your head. Consider your source.

The 5 Phases Of Dating

If you must speak with someone other than a Marriage and Family Therapist or a Couples Counselor, talk to a friend that is happily married or one that is in a healthy relationship. Find out what their secret has been. Ask for pointers from a source that can attest to living through the challenges of a marriage and coming out on top, not nay-sayers and others that change relationships, husbands, and lovers like they change clothes. Unless you want to become a new member of the LTL committee, be very careful about whom you allow into your business.

Never Lose Sight Of Who You Are As An Individual!!!

Once you are married, start having children and family responsibilities, it is easy to lose sight of who you are. To forget the things that made you happy after years of putting your needs on the back burner for the sake of the family.

Always keep some sort of activity going on the side. Whether it's taking a class, meeting your girlfriends for lunch, dinner or drinks; maybe even taking up a new hobby. It doesn't matter what it is as long as you have something that brings you happiness outside of your marriage. There will be times when you are so exhausted of taking care of everyone else that you are ready to hit a wall. In those times, if you have your "happy place" you can go there to recharge your battery and come back to your family nice and refreshed; with your love cup full again.

Anita M. Charlot

You NEED this and once you have it, all of the other minor bumps in the road won't seem as difficult to maneuver.

PART 4: DIFFERENCES BETWEEN DATING AS A WOMAN VS. A GROWN-ASS WOMAN

Anita M. Charlot

On the pages that follow, you will find charts that show the difference in how a woman approaches dating and how a Grown-Ass Woman approaches dating. The comparisons are in no way meant to throw shade on either party but instead to point out the differences when a woman has taken the time to do the work necessary to learn how to date from a healthier place. The challenge that we have been presented with as women is that we do not often learn these things while dating and relating in our younger years unless we have been raised by or around women that were comfortable in their own skin and shared these differences with us. That didn't happen for me and so I had to learn the hard way.

I'd like you to take a look at the charts that follow. See how many scenarios you can find yourself in. The number itself will be irrelevant, the goal however, is to bring your awareness to your past dating habits and show you how a Grown-Ass Woman would do it instead. Of course this is only scratching the surface of what is possible based on the woman's emotional and spiritual evolution. There will be certain situations a Grown-Ass Woman may need to handle these things differently so I would use these as a guidepost pointing you in the direction of a more confident and authentic way of dating.

The 5 Phases Of Dating

Topics	Woman	Grown-Ass Woman
Past Experiences		
Accepts her past experiences and behaviors	Every woman has a past, past behaviors that she is not proud of, past experiences that she wishes never happened or those that she can't forget. These experiences, if looked at from the proper perspective, will allow her to get extremely clear on the spirit of the man that is right for her based on what she truly wants.	This woman is not controlled by her past experiences and behaviors. She has grown through them. She has identified where she fell short and where she allowed her past to cause her to accept relationships that were not the best for her, or to even accept disrespectful behavior because she felt she didn't deserve something different.
Accepts her relationship past	Women say things like, *I don't need a relationship. I don't need a man. I'm in a relationship with B.O.B.- a battery-operated boyfriend.* This is a result of residual energy from past relationships and constantly moving from one relationship to another. Even if there was distance, without doing the healing work, leaves a woman with a bad taste in her mouth. One that either causes her to put up a hard exterior when dating so that she cannot be hurt	A **Grown-Ass Woman** recognizes that she should work through her past residual energy. She realizes that until she gets the remnants out of her mind and heart from her previous relationships that every dating or relationship experience from that point on will have been tainted. She wants an authentic relationship. She wants to love again, to trust again, and so, she puts in the work.

	again, or one that causes her to remain alone with a life supply of batteries.	
Accepts her role in her previous relationships	Women play the victim when they have been hurt in relationships. They feel say things like, *He didn't appreciate me. He didn't understand me. He never gave me what I wanted. He cheated on me, repeatedly. He continuously lied to me.* Often, it's so much easier to blame the other person versus taking responsibility for our own actions and the role we played in allowing those things to take place.	A **Grown-Ass Woman** does the work to assess what worked and what didn't work in her past relationships. She openly acknowledges the role she played, takes responsibility for her own happiness, and learns how to date and relate from that place of wholeness, having learned healthy boundaries. She no longer claims the title of victim, but rather, victory. Once she has freed her spirit and her mind and accepted the role she played, the memories and the energy of those past relationships no longer have control over her.
The Way She Treats Her Man		
Allows a grown man to be who he is	As women, it is in our nature to want the best for others; that includes our men. This often blurs the lines between being his woman versus being his mother. As women, we can see the potential in the men	A Grown-Ass Woman recognizes that if she is going to be with a man, she needs to accept him for who he is, in the beginning. She takes the time to get to know what she wants, what it looks like *and* what it

The 5 Phases Of Dating

	that we date, and we often want to help them become the man that we know he could be.	feels like so that she dates smarter from the beginning. She no longer dates a man for his unlimited potential, but for who he is at the moment of their introduction, and if there are things that they can help each other with, then it's from a different place entirely.
Allows a grown man to make his own mistakes	It is our tendency to want to stop others from making the same mistakes that we did. We can see the train wreck happening, and instead of allowing it to do so, we want to do whatever we can to stop it. This can truly backfire when it comes to our men. For example, let's say your man is responsible for the light bill. You see the disconnect notices come in the mail, and you are waiting patiently for him to pay it. You mention it casually and he says he's going to take care of it, but you do not see it happening and then **poof**-you wake up in the middle of the night	A **Grown-Ass Woman** sees what's about to happen and waits for **lights out**. She prepares for it by buying flashlights and candles. When the lights go out, she doesn't curse, argue, or get upset. She knows what's at stake here. She knows how embarrassed he must be, but recognizes that if she bails him out this time, she removes the lesson. So, what does she do? She makes do with the situation. She orders in, sets up dinner by candlelight, and does her best to make the situation bearable until **he** figures out what to do. Once he makes this mistake, he will **never** make it

	to a completely dark house.	again. He will also **never** forget how she handled the situation, or how she showed him support, and didn't make him feel worse than he did already, by allowing him as the man to make the decision.
Allows a man to be a man	Unless a man grew up in a household full of sisters or female relatives, he is not going to come with a true understanding of the feminine energy. A woman expects her man to talk to her like her girlfriends do, listening to her complain about the same stuff repeatedly, like her friends do, or even responding to her in conversation the way her friends do. This is unrealistic.	A **Grown-Ass Woman** understands men's energy. She knows how to communicate to her man so that he can hear and understand her. She knows how to interpret his comments and non-verbal responses so that they are on the same page. She realizes what she can expect to receive from him and what she should look to her girlfriends for. She's done her homework on learning the energy of men and understands how to work within that energy for the growth of her relationship with him.
Allows him to forge his own spiritual path	If spirituality is important to you as a woman, then you need to be very careful about not pushing the man that you are with to go	A **Grown-Ass Woman** understands this. She knows that the man that she intends to be with is her spiritual equal. They believe in

The 5 Phases Of Dating

	to church or be something that he is not so that he can fit in your world. If what you want is a man that is spiritual or a man that believes in God as you do, then he should come that way before you commit to each other.	the same thing or at least in a higher power. She allows him to have his very own relationship with God as she has hers. She doesn't push him to do things her way, and she has a clear understanding of what spirit or religion means to him.
Makes him feel included	When a woman gives birth to a baby, a degree, a new career, or an entrepreneurial pursuit, she tends to put all her focus there. She wants whatever it is to be successful, and therefore, doesn't realize that she is taking time away from her man and making him feel excluded. Plenty of men state that they feel like a third or fourth wheel as their women put kids and other responsibilities before them.	A **Grown-Ass Woman** finds a way to make her man feel included. Even if he cannot be included in her pursuits directly, she sets aside specific time that allows him to be patient, because he knows his time is coming, and realizes he is still important. She has also determined what makes him feel included when he can't have her one-on-one attention as she recognizes that men crave attention to.
Recognizes his contributions and celebrates them	A woman turns into a complaining machine when her man doesn't wash the dishes, clothes, or car the way she likes it. She doesn't realize how difficult it must be for a man to	A **Grown-Ass Woman** recognizes that the way to get what she wants from her man is to celebrate the behaviors that she likes. Acknowledge what he does, thank him, make

	keep all the things that she likes, as well as all the other women in his life in perspective? He tries. He misses. He gets shot down. He tries again. He doesn't bring the right brand of milk home, and he's "in trouble." He doesn't remember a special date, and she yells and screams at him.	a big deal of it, and then watch him do more to get that same response from you again. She knows how to encourage him to do things the way she wants them done in a way that doesn't demean his actions or make him feel like a failure.
Dates the whole man	Often, women will date a man with potential feeling, as though it would be easier for them to build a boyfriend. They find the man that is struggling, and they attempt to raise him into the man they've always wanted. Maybe he said he wanted to own a business one day. That impresses her, and she sees a future with the two of them being in business together. So, she begins to do all the research. She signs them both up for the seminars, makes the initial calls, sets up the meeting, and then gets angry when he doesn't seem to be as into it as she is. After all, it was his idea to begin with.	Words alone do not move **Grown-Ass Woman**. Even if she would love to have a man that she could be in business with, she doesn't date potential. She hears what he says, and she watches what he does. She is not impressed by conversation, but by actions. She knows that it is common practice to meet the representative in the beginning and dates long enough to see if he is, in fact, the man he presented himself to be in the beginning. And if she doesn't like what she sees, if she notices that he is not as driven as she is in certain areas, or if she recognizes that it is just not going to

The 5 Phases Of Dating

	She then starts telling him what he should be doing. She treats him like her child, fusses at him for not "doing his homework," and then loses interest in intimacy because he is not doing what he said he wanted to do.	work, she has no problem walking away. She has a full life with her very own goals that she has worked hard to achieve, and while she doesn't mind helping a brother with his dream, she is not going to live out that dream for him.
Allows a man to be a man	Women try to dictate what a man does, how he does it, and when he does it. This is not how you should behave in a relationship. I hear women all the time complaining about what he won't do and how she must tell him what to do. Then, they wonder why he doesn't take the initiative to do anything anymore. If you do not trust that he is man enough to handle the responsibilities, then why are you with him in the first place? If what you want is a man, then you must be willing to allow him to be a man, even if that means allowing him to make a mistake that he will eventually learn from. Being in a dating situation or a	A **Grown-Ass Woman** knows what she is looking for in a man, and therefore, removes the necessity to raise the man she is dating. She knows what a **Grown-Ass Man** looks like to her and this is who she chooses to date. She understands that there will be times that she will not agree with his methods, his process, or his decisions, but that they are his to make. If she is purely dating, or they are simply in a relationship, then she recognizes if his decisions do not put her in harm's way, it's really none of her business. He is free to make his own decisions however he pleases. She is paying close attention to the decisions he

	relationship is not a license for you to tell him how to live his life. There will be times when you will need to provide input, but not allowing him to make his own decisions is a recipe for disaster long term. You will eventually grow tired of having to always take the lead and will eventually become resentful. You will begin to see him as a child and then lose respect for him.	makes, how he makes them, and whether his way of doing things are in alignment with hers. Knowing this, as time goes on, she benefits from allowing him to be the man, because it releases her responsibility to always lead everything. If her idea of a relationship is a traditional one, where the man is the head of household (once they are in the same house), she has identified how to have a "traditional relationship" without having to give up her strength.
Matches spirits, not résumés	A woman believes that matching résumés equal compatibility in relationships. This isn't true. If you're an ambitious woman that is highly decorated in the community or your industry, then this doesn't mean that the man that you are in a relationship with must have a matching résumé. Your friends, family members, and peers may expect you to be with a man who has accomplished just as	A **Grown-Ass Woman** attracts a man who is compatible with her spirit not necessarily her résumé. She has identified what's truly important to her and has determined that it doesn't have to come in a matching package equal to hers. She has done the work and has determined that as a well-accomplished woman outside of the home, having a man to come home to that is a compliment to her life,

The 5 Phases Of Dating

	much as you have, but is that really what you want? Are you still single because you are waiting for the right "résumé" to come along?	makes love to her heart, and supports her endeavors is far more important than a man with a matching résumé. And if this is the type of man that will in fact feed her spirit, then she knows what that looks like and is comfortable with all that his "résumé" brings with it.
Understands the importance of loving herself completely...first!	**Is Self-Aware** A woman uses compliments as validation for who she is. She doesn't understand that no number of compliments from a man will ever be enough if she does not love who she is. Not doing so will cause her to be susceptible to his mood swings (yes, they do have them). If he's in a good mood, then you will be in a good mood. If he is in a bad mood, then you will automatically think that it is because of something that you did or did not do. You will internalize his behavior, which will keep you hungry for any sense of affection from him.	A **Grown-Ass Woman** loves herself, unconditionally. She loves herself so much that what she receives from a man is extra. She is aware of her actions, her moods and when she is or is not a part of a situation. She is confident enough to allow him time to find the words to share. She is talented enough in relationship communication to teach him how to open up to her when he is "feeling some type of way."

Accepts her shadow side	Every woman has a good and a not so good side. She often tries to suppress her shadow side, which in turn causes her to have outbursts, moments of fits, and adult temper tantrums. You would recognize this part of you if you've ever said, *I was such a bitch*. This is a result of unresolved emotional energy and bad memories that are blocking you from receiving the love you want.	A **Grown-Ass Woman** accepts her shadow side. She embraces it, so much so, that she becomes one with it, understanding what she needs to work on to transform any past residual energy so that it no longer has control over her dating and relationships experiences. She grabs that energy by the balls and cuts off its circulation, thereby removing the ability of her past to dictate her present or future relationship experiences.
Discovers what her spirit needs	Women don't get what they want because they don't **know** what they want. There is a huge difference between what a woman thinks she needs and what she **really** needs. She says she wants one thing when she needs something else. You will be able to spot her within your friends, even yourself if you've ever heard or stated this phrase, *No one ever understands me*.	A **Grown-Ass Woman** knows what she wants in a relationship. She knows the things she *Must Have*, the things she *Can Compromise On* and the *Hell Naws* (deal breakers). She uses these things to pre-qualify her dating prospects and to learn how to articulate her needs at the appropriate time.

The 5 Phases Of Dating

Knows that she does want a man	Women uses phrases like, *I don't need a man.* When I hear women say this, what they really mean is *I've been so hurt and disappointed in the past that I refuse to feel that pain again. Can you hear that? I can do bad all by myself. Why would I allow some man to come into my life and tell me what to do? All men are dogs. All men cheat, so why even bother being in a relationship?* Having been in the game for nearly twenty years, I recognize that this is a woman's pain talking. This is a defense mechanism that she uses to keep from being hurt and disappointed all over again. What she doesn't realize is that it's this very way of thinking that is keeping her single.	A **Grown-Ass Woman** no longer uses these phrases. She understands that the energy behind her words block her ability to have the love she wants. It is a mental and emotional repellent. She took the time to learn where the pain was, why it was there, and how she can heal from it. And then, she learned ways a man could compliment her life. As a result, she began to attract the quality of man that was perfectly imperfect for her. As the quality of prospects improved, so did the quality of dating and relationship experiences.
Knows that all attention is not good attention.	When a woman is missing something, there is something that she feels that she is lacking: beauty, body, brains, money, degrees, or accomplishments. If	This woman has learned what those things are, has grown through them and is not moved by the compliments of the first guy that comes along.

	she feels she's missing something, she is open to falling for the first man that pays her any attention. If he gives her a compliment that touches on what she lacks, then she's hooked.	This doesn't mean that he is lying or that she should not appreciate his compliments. It simply means his compliments do not cause her to fall immediately. She is able to focus on other parts of his conversation to discover more about him.
Relationship Behavior		
Never plays 2nd	Women knowingly play 2nd or become side pieces, which keeps them in that position. If you met your man in the middle of a relationship with another woman, how can you trust that he will not meet another woman in the middle of yours?	A **Grown-Ass Woman** will **never** play 2nd to anyone. Even if he states that he is in the middle of a divorce, she realizes that she should wait until he completes his divorce, and then has the time to work through his emotional issues and co-parenting agreements before he's ready to start another serious relationship. She realizes she runs the risk of being the rebound person if she doesn't.
Releases the need to feel in control	Women who have been hurt in the past will often demonstrate a need to control what happens around them. It doesn't matter whether the pain is from their childhood,	A **Grown-Ass Woman** knows that trying to control every aspect of her life will never work, especially her relationships. She also knows that while she should have standards

The 5 Phases Of Dating

	or an intimate relationship, feeling **out of control**, if not properly addressed, puts her in a defensive position. The way women often deal with this is by **attempting** to control their environments. Things must be a certain way. Their mates must behave in a certain way for them to not feel like they are losing their footing.	and boundaries, expecting others to tip toe around her feelings and do exactly what she **needs** them to do so that she feels safe, is not realistic. She does not expect the other person to change who they are to be with her. She takes her time getting to know the truth of who that person really is and determines if they would be a good fit for one another, sharing their likes and dislikes in a healthy way.
Is equally yoked with her partner	Women believe that being unequally yoked only applies to religion. But, this concept also becomes a problem when women have not identified what the spirit of the person that they want to be with **looks and feels like.** For example, if you want someone that is health conscious, then when dating, you should look for things that they do naturally that show that they are health conscious. Do they talk about healthy ways of eating? Do they go to the gym?	A **Grown-Ass Woman** takes the time to identify the spirit of the person that is perfectly-imperfect for her. If being healthy is something that is important for her, she will listen for **healthy conscious comments** from potential suitors. She will watch how they respond to her if she has expressed a desire to be healthier. Do they choose healthy restaurants? Do they hide the potato chips when she goes to their house? How do they show their support

		without her having to ask? Because she knows what is important to her and what to look for, she recognizes this upfront without having to spend unnecessary time, energy, and emotions.
Takes time in between relationships to identify the lessons	Women who fear being alone make bad relationship choices. They don't like being alone. They don't like the dating game, and therefore, they tend to jump into relationships too soon, not having taken the time to review the previous relationships and identified the lessons it taught. I get it. It's hard to face the fact that **you** may be the reason you continue to attract the wrong type of person. Maybe it feels better to see yourself as the victim, and so you refuse to go within to see why this keeps happening to you. Continue to move forward without the introspection, and you will continue to relive the same relationship drama, with more	A **Grown-Ass Woman** takes the time to do a **self-check**. She takes the time to heal her heart, identify the lesson(s), and then course correct as she opens her heart for the next dating and/or relationship experience. She understands that if she continues to attract the same type of relationships into her life, the only constant in her relationship equation is her. She is actively participating. To attract better, she must become better at identifying what works, what didn't work, and why. Once she has identified those things, she can then move forward with healing, learning, course correcting, and attracting the quality of love that she wants. As

The 5 Phases Of Dating

	intensified pain.	she understands how important this is, she is not in any hurry to jump into the next relationship with blinders on.
Applies practical relationship experience to book, seminar, retreat, and class knowledge	Women use comments like this to describe their relationship knowledge, *I've taken ten classes about dating and relationships. I've read over twenty books. I've done twelve retreats, so I am fully knowledgeable about how things work. I just need to find someone that has just as much knowledge as me.* Having amassed hours of reading, retreat/seminar training does not equal practical dating and relationship experience. Don't get me wrong. Reading is a great way to learn new concepts and discover new ways of doing/viewing dating and relationships, but it will never equal a **free pass**. Growth and true experience come from trial and error. If you were to put all that knowledge into practice with actual dating and relationship experience,	A **Grown-Ass Woman** recognizes that she doesn't need to do all of that. She doesn't need to pay thousands of dollars to several different organizations to learn about relationships. She takes the time to do a personal inventory of her life, her past relationships, her desires, and her needs, and to identify the spirit of the person that is perfectly imperfect for her. Where necessary, she works with a coach to help her along the way. Having one person that knows you, your past, your tendencies, and your desires can keep you on track and assist you with practical application. She knows that trying to date from acquired knowledge only will postpone her desire of attracting and maintaining the relationship that she

	then you would be much closer to having the relationship you've always wanted.	really wants.
Identifies the gaps in her current relationship	A woman has gaps between the relationship she has and the relationship he wants. In her past, she has asked for things and never received them, and as a result, she often accepts less than what she needs, wants, or deserves.	A **Grown-Ass Woman** knows how to identify gaps, and she works to either close the gap in her relationship, or remove herself from the relationship all together. If closing the gap requires her to seek additional help, learn new things, or accept the truth about her situation, then that's what she does. If she needs help doing so, then she seeks out help and puts in the work. If she determines that gaps will require both parties to do the work, then she's open to it and doesn't have a problem discussing this with her man.
	Strong Personality	
Is strong and fiercely independent (SAFI)	Many women are single mothers, caregivers, older siblings, and entrepreneurs. Women who play these roles, and others, have become strong and fiercely independent to keep things in order. If	A **Grown-Ass Woman** has recognized that being a SAFI doesn't mean that she must stop being who she is to have a relationship. She recognizes what her fears are, and she has addressed them head

The 5 Phases Of Dating

	she is not careful, the very same SAFI traits will work against her when trying to attract and maintain an authentic relationship. She will have a hard time allowing a man in because she doesn't want him to upset the perfect environment that she has created. She doesn't want to have to **dumb down** to keep him from feeling intimidated. She doesn't want any man telling her how she should raise her children, interact with her family, or run her business.	on. She dates from a healthy place, a place that recognizes the type of man she needs in her life, that will compliment and not complicate. She knows that the way she communicates in the other areas of her life where she is in charge is not the way she will communicate in her relationships.
Is mindful about her speech	Women like to *keep it 100*. This is the reason a lot of relationships do not work. She wants to be able to speak her mind at all times, and so, she shares everything. In the spirit of **keeping it 100** she does more damage. Look at it this way. If your mate shared everything that was on their minds with you whenever it popped into their head, how would you feel? **Keeping it 100** is an	A **Grown-Ass Woman** recognizes that there are things that come into her awareness to be shared, and there are other things that come into her awareness as information only. If she has identified something about her partner that she sees as a flaw, she understands that just because she thinks this doesn't give her the right to say it. She picks and chooses what needs to be shared based on her

	excuse that a lot of women use as a defense mechanism. Somewhere in their past, they didn't speak up, and as a result, they refuse to ever be in that position again.	understanding of herself and why she feels the need to point out her partner's flaws. There will come a time when she needs to share and when that time arises, she knows how to present it so that the other party receives it well. Because she is selective, these conversations are more effective.
Is coachable	Women put up with abuse: verbal, physical, mental, and emotional. As a result, they've built walls of toughness to protect themselves from future hurt. Women build walls so impenetrable that they can't hear those that can help them **grow through** their past. Or they connect with others based on their familiar sufferings, and the cycle continues. You see this with a group of female friends who are all single and have been for years.	A **Grown-Ass Woman** recognizes that she cannot do it alone. All the nights of crying herself to sleep and pretending not to want a relationship, which is so far to the left of what she really feels, causes her to seek out the reason. She wants to know what is standing in the way of getting the love she wants and what she needs to do to get it. She understands that this will sometimes mean that she will have to stop following the thought processes of the group and reach out to someone that can support her through her fears and insecurities.

The 5 Phases Of Dating

Doesn't take conversations personally	Women spend a ton of time trying to decipher what someone meant by their last comment. This is a waste of time. Sitting at home wondering if he's truly interested in your or if he meant what he said is more of a reflection on you than it is on him. If you must wonder about his thoughts, feelings, or actions, then there is still work for you to do on yourself. It's time for you to ask yourself, *why?* Why are you second-guessing his thoughts, words, and actions? Do you think he's lying to you? Is there trust in your relationship? Can you trust him to be a man of his word? Have you not healed from something in your past? What is **your** truth in this situation?	A **Grown-Ass Woman** doesn't waste time trying to decipher what he meant. She is confident in her communication skills, and she has identified within herself the way in which she would like for her man to act so that things are clear to her. She has also started attracting men into her life that are not elusive, that are able and willing to share their thoughts and feelings without being prodded so that she never has to guess what's going on with him. She doesn't take the things he does personally or internalize his behavior because she has a greater understanding of the spirit of men, and if she needed to ask him about an issue, she knows how to do so based on his personality.

Anita M. Charlot

FINAL THOUGHTS
✶ ☆ ✶

Whew! It's finished. It's finally done. I've given birth to two wonderful boys and the labor was nothing like that of this book. If you had any idea how many rewrites, edits, starts and stops that took to get this book to the printer, you would be exhausted.

Are you familiar with Wayne Dyer? In listening to several of his audiobooks he always says, "Don't die with your music still in you." I have carried this music with me for the past 14 years. And I was determined to let it play. Trust me. When you set your mind on a path, every obstacle imaginable will somehow magically appear. It's as though the Universe was saying, *so you want to write a book, huh? You want to share the knowledge that you've gained because of your experiences? Well, I think you need to have a few more experiences during this process. Let's see how serious you are about its completion.*

I have been tried, tested, proved wrong, embarrassed, ashamed, afraid, disappointed, deceived, terrified of success, and terrified of failure. I've run from completing the book out of that four-letter word: **fear**. Fear paralyzed my creativity and kept me running from my home office and successfully blaming this major incomplete on everyone else around me. Many books about dating have come out, while I was pregnant with this idea. I thought to myself that there was enough information already out there. If a person happened to be a bibliophile like me, then they could just join a book club and spend an entire year reading about dating.

Anita M. Charlot

Then a thought occurred to me. Each writer has their own unique way of placing their ideas and thoughts in black and white. My thoughts, while possibly similar to someone else's, are mine. There is no one person out there that has lived the life that I have experienced, or achieved the growth that I have because of my experience with being an equal opportunity dater or the many challenges that it presented, but have managed to do what I've done despite it. No other story is like that of mine and I am sincerely hoping that while the bisexual nature of the book may not suit your lifestyle, the concepts, the need to get in touch with your *Purrfectly Authentic*™ self still resonates the same. There are countless women out there that rise above all types of misfortune. This book is for you. Learning to get in touch with your *Purrfectly Authentic*™ self, your *Purrfectly Authentic*™ voice, creating your Purrfect Life Story™, and your 3 Lists will empower you to step outside of your current situation. As Wayne Dyer (2009) suggests, *You'll See It When You Believe It*.

Throughout my life, I have loved, learned, and lost many wonderful people, from friendships, relationships, marriages, and even death. But one thing remains true: I sincerely thank each and every one of them from the bottom of my heart. And for those that I have not had the opportunity to thank in person, *thank you for being a part of my soul's journey*. It is because of you, all that you were, and all that you were not that pointed me in the direction I have found myself in today.

Every now and then, I come across someone that wants to challenge my credentials. They will ask me things, such as "What certifications do you have? Where did you go to school? Are you an actual psychiatrist, LCSW, certified coach,

The 5 Phases Of Dating

or counselor? What qualifies you to lead workshops, seminars, and even one-on-one sessions?" And my answer is always the same...**life**! I do hold a coaching certification as well as a Master NLP Certification, however, they would mean nothing to my clients without the understanding of having walked in their shoes.

I have walked on both sides of the fence. I have lived through many challenging relationships. I have survived all types of abuse within my relationships. I have reared two wonderful children in the process. I have created my own business, while holding down a regular full-time job for the past eight years. I have been a part of two company downsizings. I have been passed over for promotions and not given quality raises. I have been on public aid and unemployment. I have written and published two books and working on my third. I've fought with family members. I've run away from God. I have been to hell's door and back several times and you know what? I'm still here. I'm still standing.

Truth, reality, and the ability to relate is what my clients come to me for. I would much rather take advice from someone who has experienced the pain that I did and had similar experiences, than someone who had only textbook knowledge.

I have lived through all that to finally begin to live my life being who I really am: the *Purrfectly Authentic*™ me. I know God now in a much more real sense than I knew before. Through all of this, I grew to understand the spirit of the person that I wanted in my life and I found the courage to wait for him. If I had not done all of the work on ME, I would not only have missed out on attracting such a wonderful man, but I would not have known how to keep him. He accepted me BECAUSE of the person I became due to my challenges, my dark nights of the soul, my knocks on hell's door, my welfare checks, my WIC cards, my time in the military, my divorce, and the abuse that I suffered at the hands of those who claimed to love me. In him, I found the strength to love myself more than I ever have for he has provided me a safe space to do so. At the time of this writing, we've been together 10 years and we still look at each other as though we just met. I'm still here, standing, proud of the woman that I see in his eyes every time he looks at me.

So what should you do while you wait, while you work on you? Find the words, the songs, the books, the support, the communities that help you keep your energy high, that provide you a safe space when everything else around you is falling apart. If the life that I have lived and the mess that I have grown through doesn't qualify me to be a dating and relationship coach, then I don't know what will.

Life is not always about how many letters you have behind your name, what school you went to, or what professional association you belong to. For many of us it's about making a difference. It's about sharing what we've learned with others so they understand they are not the first that has gone through their life experience, and they won't be the last. It's about showing others how to rise above their current life situation or their past, so they can create the type of future they desire. Why? How? Because there is always something more. You only need to know how to acquire it.

After all is said and done, it is my sincere hope that you will at least walk away from this book with a new way of viewing the dating experience. Even if you never do the exercises given, just having read the words on these pages

The 5 Phases Of Dating

will be enough to open up that portion of your spirit that will speak to you, telling you that you deserve more. You can have more. All you have to do is be crystal clear on what it is you want and be willing to do the work necessary in order to open your mind, your spirit, and your heart to get it.

Should you like to take your transformation deeper with an understanding of how you can progress to dating from a Grown-Ass Woman's perspective, there is a companion workbook. To learn more about the workbook, please go to www.anitacharlot.com.

To Your Dating and Relationship Success
Your Coach, Anita Charlot

Anita M. Charlot

AFTERWORD

✯ ☆ ✯

Whether explicitly or implicitly, we are taught to seek guidance from our mothers, fathers, sisters, brothers, and friends well before relying on ourselves. Over time, this causes many of us to distrust our own internal guidance systems, leaving us to flounder in the murky relationship advice of others, which is oftentimes based on someone else's own fears and bad experiences.

Luckily, Anita Charlot has provided us with sound counsel worth delving into well before even agreeing to date number one. *The 5 Phases of Dating* provides an unconventional take on how to be in relationship not only with another person, but also with one's self.

Anita's analogy comparing a relationship to building a home is brilliant. And when you think about it that way, it only makes sense that the foundation is you. I've been married for over twenty years to the same person, and it wasn't until five years ago that I realized our relationship was wobbly because I didn't know myself. I had to do as Anita says in *Internal Groundwork* and establish who I was first. Had I been given the questions she asks, made a list, or understood the 3-6-9 rule years ago, perhaps, my marriage would've begun with a concrete frame.

After we've gotten ourselves together, Anita makes clear that just because we know ourselves doesn't mean that we should jump head first into a committed relationship. Phases I-V show women how to slow things down. With Phase I, readers learn how to develop a friendship and get to know the other person. This is key. I've had many friends meet, date, and marry their mates within six months' time. All those relationships have ended in divorce. While every relationship is different, Phase I provides you with sample questions that support your taking time to get to know the person before you dive into a full-on relationship.

Phase II is the most progressive part of Anita's dating steps. Similar to not being taught to listen to ourselves, we're also discouraged from dating around. But this is exactly what Anita suggests. However, she clearly explains how to maneuver this step with respect that will lead to success. Though this might sound taboo, especially for women, readers are not encouraged to sleep around, but rather consider different relationship options, while being honest with each potential partner. Readers aren't left to believe these are idealistic concepts. Anita illustrates every piece of advice with her own past relationship examples.

Effective communication and knowing one's boundaries are integral for Phase III. Once we begin dating someone exclusively, our minds jump directly to marriage. One of the best pieces of advice from this phase is "The first thing we need to cover is the fact that you are in a *relationship*, not married." Being married to someone comes with a different list of expectations and privileges than being in a committed relationship. Anita's lists of questions might seem daunting, but sorting out specifics

The 5 Phases Of Dating

will help communicate clear expectations and guidelines at the onset, which may save heartache in the end.

Anita outlines how to move to a more permanent state of relationship with Phases IV and V. Much of the success of these two phases rely on two people conversing about maintaining their "house" both literally and figuratively. Once in a permanent relationship, partners must determine a respectful living arrangement; likewise, figuratively it is imperative that each person also teaches outsiders (e.g., family and friends) how to respect the new relationship. Should one make it to Phase V, then a deeper level of communication and understanding are required.

Kudos to Anita Charlot for publishing the second edition of *The 5 Phases of Dating*! It is timely. Unlike other self-help books, there is no finger wagging at women and all they must do to independently create and maintain successful relationships. This book is for everyone who consciously wants to co-create loving partnerships. Anita does an excellent job of demonstrating that all unions begin with one person, our self. Although it's a simple concept, it is quite revolutionary to learn that *all* relationship issues can be resolved by getting clear about one's self, and then vibing out from there. This might not be the advice we want to hear, but it is definitely the advice we need to hear.

Dr. K E Garland
Author of *The Unhappy Wife*
http://www.kegarland.com/

www.ingramcontent.com/pod-product-compliance
Lightning Source LLC
Chambersburg PA
CBHW071422160426
43195CB00013B/1775